Medieval Chinese Society and the Local "Community"

Tanigawa Michio

Medieval Chinese Society and the Local "Community"

Translated, with an Introduction, by Joshua A. Fogel

UNIVERSITY OF CALIFORNIA PRESS
Berkeley   Los Angeles   London

University of California Press
Berkeley and Los Angeles, California

University of California Press, Ltd.
London, England

Copyright © 1985 by
The Regents of the University of California

Library of Congress Cataloging in Publication Data

Tanigawa, Michio, 1925–
    Medieval Chinese society and the local "community".

    Translation of: Chūgoku chūsei shakai to kyōdōtai.
    Includes index.
    1. China—Social conditions—221 B.C.–960 A.D.
I. Fogel, Joshua A., 1950–   . II. Title.
HN733.T3613   1985   306′.0931   84-28024
ISBN 0-520-05370-2

Printed in the United States of America

1   2   3   4   5   6   7   8   9

To Professor Kawakatsu Yoshio (1922–1984) who passed
away while this translation was being prepared.

Contents

Translator's Introduction

Stagnation, Feudalism, and Periodization

Although Japanese scholarship on Chinese history reached stunning heights of intellectual discovery and erudition in the early decades of this century, in the eyes of postwar academics Japanese military aggression on the Asian mainland has tainted much of prewar scholarly efforts. Most major scholarly enterprises—an obvious example being the Research Bureau of the South Manchurian Railway Company or Mantetsu[a]—were funded by the same government that pursued the military occupation of China. Many scholars either approved Japan's invasion or silently left "politics" to the "politicians." Only an infinitesimally small minority in Japan, in any field, openly disputed their nation's claims in Asia. It was far more common for scholars either to say nothing and use the guise of nationally funded research to do fieldwork in China—as in the case of many Mantetsu researchers—or to justify Japanese advances into Asia for reasons of "history," "national fate," or "national necessity"—as in the cases of Yano Jin'ichi,[b] Inoue Tetsujirō,[c] and Shionoya On.[d]

Scholarship in the postwar period has been dominated in Japan by Marxists of varying inclinations but intent as a group on purging the prewar demons from their midst. This has entailed a long battle with the tremendous guilt arising from the knowledge that prewar sinologists went along with military aggression, openly or passively, and displayed a deep contempt for China and her people. Why did sinologists, they ask, so badly misunderstand the nature of Chinese history and society?

One widespread academic direction has been against the notion, identified with prewar Japanese sinology, that China was ageless and demonstrated no historical development—that is, a static conception of China's past. This response has led to debates on the periodization of Chinese history, for once the

various eras in the Marxist schema of historical development
could be plotted for China, she would then be shown to have a
history no different from that of any other country. Particularly, focus has been directed at identifying the parameters of
China's feudal period and the essence of Chinese feudalism. As
Niida Noboru[e] passionately explained in a brilliant essay first
published in 1946, the very act of proper periodization, the
assignment on the basis of research of the feudal period in
Chinese history—the period that was in the process of being
overcome ever since the Taipings, according to Niida—was
itself an attack on stagnationist conceptions.[1] Periodization
along Marxist lines thus became a task that sought to redress
Japan's debt to China by rehumanizing the Japanese view of
Chinese history.

The great majority of Japanese scholars, even the non-
Marxists, felt deeply sympathetic to the rebellious and revolutionary activities of the Chinese people in the century from
the Taiping Rebellion through the victory of the Communist
revolution in 1949. These events themselves constituted proof
to contradict any notion of a passive, undynamic nation; and
they necessitated a search farther back into Chinese history to
assess fully the "feudal" period which, over this past century,
was finally being overcome.

Why Japanese scholars have spent so much time and energy
on the issue of feudalism deserves some consideration. For
Marxist scholars, feudalism itself was an issue, the source from
whence emerges capitalism (under which most academic Marxists were living). A people might skip the capitalist stage of
development, according to some theorists, but no people ever
skipped the feudal stage of societal development.

Feudalism as a more general historiographic problem had
specific import for Japan. Virtually every modern Japanese
scholar has the Meiji Restoration of 1868 looming in his or her
consciousness as a distinct model for the orthodox transcendence of feudalism or the failure to do so. Be that for better or
for worse—and most Japanese Marxists regard the legacy of
the Meiji Restoration as a two-edged sword at best—the issue
of feudalism has occupied a central position in their thoughts.
The failure of the Meiji reforms to transcend Japanese feudalism has repeatedly been blamed for the lingering feudal ele-

ments (or remnants) that played such a heinous role in the 1930s and 1940s when the military was ascendant. Had feudalism been fully sublated, many scholars argue, the Japanese might not have had to go through that frightful and destructive era.[2]

To a certain extent, Japanese scholars have projected this concern (or obsession, perhaps) with feudalism onto Chinese historical research, although historians from the People's Republic of China are equally obsessed with feudalism and periodization. Similarly, Japanese studies of the French Revolution, the quintessential bourgeois-democratic revolution, often involve intricate comparisons with the Meiji Restoration, as in some of the work of Kuwabara Takeo, Kobayashi Yoshiaki, and Inoue Kōji.[3]

The problem of stagnationist theories and of reassessing Chinese history in such a way as to afford China the same principles of historical development as the West was considerably deeper than at first conceived. The Italian historian Frederico Chabod (whose work has been translated into Japanese but not into English as yet)[4] has shown that the idea of "Europe" itself emerged from a self-comparison with Asia in Greek times. Europe (i.e., the Greeks) was represented by the spirit of freedom, Asia by despotism, with a conscious separation intended. By extension, it was argued, European freedom was linked to progress, whereas Asian despotism had resulted in stagnation. This idea, according to Chabod, was revived in the eighteenth century by thinkers from Montesquieu to Voltaire. With the Enlightenment, capitalist production, the development of ideas of political democracy, science, and the like all contributed to strengthen this Europocentric world historical conception. These distinguishing notions—freedom vs. despotism, progress vs. stagnation—became inseparably linked to Europe's concept of its own modernity. Namely, where there is "modernity," one can find concomitant freedom and progress; but, where there are difficulties that crop up on the road to modernization, there one will be able to point to despotism and stagnation.

Nonetheless, to demonstrate that Chinese history was not simply the rise and fall of despotic empires, Japanese sinologists set out to provide Chinese history with an image no different from that of the West or Japan. China, too, it would be shown, had gone through the universally applicable stages of ancient slavery, medieval feudalism, and modern capitalism. In this way China would be integrated into an evolving world history. One of the first efforts in this regard, discussed by Tanigawa Michio,[f] was the notorious case of Nishijima Sadao.[g] In a 1950 essay, Nishijima argued that slavery was the mode of production that characterized Chinese society under the Ch'in-Han Empire. After a critical rebuttal from such scholars as Masubuchi Tatsuo,[h] Nishijima was compelled later to reassess this hasty appraisal and eventually to withdraw it altogether.[5]

The mechanical application of labels to different periods in Chinese history as a means of identifying historical development began to run aground of its own accord in the mid- to late 1950s. Tanigawa Michio raised his doubts in public about the label "ancient" for T'ang at the 1955 annual meeting of the Rekishigaku kenkyūkai,[i] the established Marxist organization of historians in Japan. In a 1961 essay and later in his surveys of Japanese research for 1961 and 1966 on the Six Dynasties period, Tanigawa expressed concern at the lack of scholarly productivity caused by the intellectual strangulation of a predetermined periodization.[6] Tanigawa had himself followed the general trend in believing that the Sui-T'ang marked the close of Chinese antiquity, but no one had yet offered detailed and empirical studies of the institutional issues involved here to substantiate the theory. Before one could designate a priori a name for the Sui-T'ang era, should not one first have asked: "What happened during the Sui-T'ang?" "What reality gave form to its historical world?" For, if the task before Japanese sinology was to integrate Chinese history into world history, how could one ignore such questions, Tanigawa wondered.[7]

There was another critical problem Tanigawa noted. The Marxist periodization also assumed that the state in the "ancient" Sui-T'ang era was inseparable from its institutions; substructure and superstructure were inextricably united. Institutions were merely the means by which the state controlled its main object, the masses of the people, but there was no significant component at the root of these institutions. Because this identification remained at the level of a presupposition, no penetrating studies were forthcoming from Marxist historians in the 1950s in Sui-T'ang institutional history, according to Tanigawa. For example, the T'ang legal code (*lü-li*)[j] was assumed to support a "slave" society, but when one separated it from the Marxist assignment of the "ancient-slave" label, it certainly appeared to have remarkably feudal elements. Without understanding the nature of the link between the people and the state, Tanigawa came to believe, it would be impossible to understand the nature of a subsequent break or opposition between them, as occurred so fiercely at the end of the T'ang. So, he began to do research on the pre-Sui state and society—namely, the Northern Wei dynasty—as a means of studying the formative process of Sui and T'ang. He has since devoted twenty or more years to this long period of division in Chinese history, principally to the houses that held sway for varying numbers of years in the North.

The Six Dynasties Period in Chinese History

The period from the fall of the Latter Han dynasty through imperial reunification under the Sui and T'ang, a period of nearly four centuries, has until recently attracted little in the way of historical research in the West. While the literature and religion of this long interregnum have received scholarly attention, historical studies lag behind.[8]

This era, known as Wei-Chin-Nan-Pei-ch'ao[k] (Wei, Chin, and Northern and Southern dynasties) or more handily as the Six Dynasties, was for a long time seen as a kind of black hole in Chinese history for several reasons. First, the difficulties posed by studying China at a time when no state held control over the entire empire seemed overwhelming. Sources abound but they are often corrupted; constant warfare, attacks from the North and conquests by people of non-Chinese origin, institutions established, but with questionable authority, all militated against the development of a clear picture of the Chinese state and society in these years. Second, traditional Chinese historiography was essentially political history, and the lack of central imperial authority constituted a giant lacuna (and, consequently, a possible source of embarrassment) in a history that otherwise boasted great dynasties usually punctuated by only short intervals. As a result, the Six Dynasties era came to be regarded as a Chinese analogue of the Dark Ages in Europe after the fall of the Roman Empire, a time when no significant intellectual advances could be cited, certainly none worthy of serious study—and, like the Dark Ages in Europe, the Six Dynasties were not studied in depth.

That such a view of China is bankrupt no longer requires a great deal of contemplation or extensive explanation. Though China suffered four centuries of political disorder, Chinese history and culture made significant advances. This was the period when the mass migrations from North China, due to the "barbarian" invasions from farther North, caused the spread of Han Chinese society and culture into South China. This development would have repercussions through all of subsequent Chinese history. South China has for the past millennium been seen as the center of Chinese culture, society, population, and the economy. In the Han dynasty, though, the South was only sparsely populated by ethnic Chinese and was still largely jungle land.

The move south by so many men and women from the North brought along the importation of Northern sedentary agricultural ways. Unlike the North, however, South China could boast extraordinary potential riches in agricultural production. The coming of metallic agricultural implements to the South and the phenomenal socioeconomic development of Kiangnan by the time the Sui and T'ang dynasties reunified China, would have enabled the South, in the words of Kawakatsu Yoshio, to jump right into the tenth century had it not had to contend with military pressures from the North.[9] Who knows what advances Kiangsu, Chekiang, or the whole of South China might have made if they had not been compelled to feed the rest of China?

The invasions of Hsiung-nu,[l] Hsien-pi,[m] and others into North China provided the opportunity for the first Sino-barbarian cooperation in the building of regimes, one of which, the Sui, eventually reunited China. We can see the remarkable attraction of many Chinese ways to these previously nomadic peoples once they conquered and occupied some part of China. Almost always they realized the necessity of relinquishing nomadic ways for sedentary agriculture, and often even the need to afford the military a secondary role in a society stressing the civil arts. These two met with considerable consternation, resistance, and occasionally civil war, but ultimately won out.

So thoroughly "civilized" did the previously martial and nomadic Northern Wei become that they made lasting contributions to Chinese society and agriculture of a distinctly civil bent—the *fu-ping*[n] or militia system for compulsory military service, as opposed to a professional army, and the *chün-t'ien*[o] or equitable field system for the fair parceling of arable land by the state.

The forerunner of the examination system, the primary route to official power throughout the last one thousand or more years of Chinese history, got its start in the early third century under the state of Wei created by Ts'ao Ts'ao.[p] This system, the *chiu-p'in chung-cheng*[q] (Nine Ranks and Arbiter), has been studied in great depth elsewhere and needs no further discussion here.[10]

We also see the growth and efflorescence of Chinese culture in the Six Dynasties period. Calligraphy and painting emerge as artistic forms, while new poetic styles and the compilation of the *Wen-hsüan*[r] poetry collection appear. And, because Confucianism was not predominant, we see an age in which a freer atmosphere existed for other religions and schools of thought, such as Buddhism and Taoism.

One remarkable difference between the Six Dynasties and the so-called Dark Ages in Europe is that, while both witness the preponderance of military types because of ceaseless warfare, the military in China proved unable to form a dominant social class, even in the warrior states of the North, through which to rule over China. It might be possible militarily to create a state, even to make oneself emperor. But to rule China, or any part of it, almost always required educated bureaucrats, and in the process the "military" rulers became "civilized." This process was particularly troubling in the North where racial antagonisms often flared.

The first scholar to delve into the morass of materials for the Six Dynasties and to emerge with a conceptual understanding of this era was Naitō Konan,[s] one of the giants of prewar Japanese sinology and a founder of the Kyoto school.[11] In a celebrated article entitled "Gaikatsuteki Tō-Sō jidai kan" (A comprehensive look at the T'ang-Sung period),[12] Naitō offered his periodization of "medieval China," which corresponded roughly to the third through the ninth centuries. He also described the characteristics of medieval culture and society, which set it off from the subsequent "modern" or "early modern" era (Sung and thereafter). Although the latter part of this periodization, that the Sung dynasty commences the "modern" (*kinsei*)[^l] era in Chinese history, is the more famous, Naitō invested considerable time into research on the middle period.

In Naitō's overall scheme, China's antiquity was a period of the emergence and flowering of Chinese culture, as well as its flow to the neighboring states on China's periphery. As this period came to a close in the late Latter Han, the outward flow of Chinese influence came to a halt. The alien peoples along China's borders, particularly in the North, having become racially aware of their own non-Chineseness by virtue of the confrontation with China, now reacted against a much weaker Chinese state. They built kingdoms in the North and were in continual strife with influences and forces from the South where so many Han Chinese had emigrated. Naitō characterized this middle era as "aristocratic" because, he argued, the society and culture were dominated by a peculiarly Chinese aristocracy, not based in land or military might or wealth, but in letters.[^13]

Several Japanese scholars who continued to work in this area were Okazaki Fumio, Utsunomiya Kiyoyoshi, and Miyakawa Hisayuki, all graduates of Kyoto University and intellectual disciples of Naitō Konan. Miyakawa also contributed the first essay in English on Naitō and his theories.[^14] Okazaki worked on a wide variety of topics, particularly social and economic institutions, but cultural history as well. Miyakawa has also studied issues in social, political, economic, and especially religious history. The importance of Utsunomiya's work on society and culture in the Six Dynasties period is discussed by Tanigawa in the body of the volume here translated.

No serious debate over Naitō's periodization occurred until after World War II, especially after the victory of the Chinese revolution in 1949, when a freer atmosphere existed in Japan and new issues appeared on the scholarly agenda. Naitō Konan became the object of scholarly invective as he too was associated with a concept of stagnation—that is, if the "modern" period began way back in the Sung and continued through till the present, then the events of the nineteenth and twentieth centuries held no special significance, for the institutions of Sung had already set the stage for what was to come.[^15]

The Six Dynasties and the "Community"

Not everyone in the scholarly world concurred in the attack on Naitō Konan, but a number of years would pass before there emerged a sustained critique of the Marxist rejoinder to Naitō and of the Marxist emplotment of Chinese history along universal lines of developmental stages. In the process of studying the wealth of sources relevant to research on the Six Dynasties period—historical, literary, philosophical, and poetic—Tanigawa and his colleague at Kyoto University, Kawakatsu Yoshio, began to develop their own theory of Chinese society at that time, a theory that did not deny classes and conflict but sought first to look at the society and draw conclusions from the evidence. They shared with most Japanese sinologists a common concern that, in addressing this period in Chinese history, one try to understand history developmentally. Thus, periodization itself was not discarded, only significantly reformulated.

Tanigawa and Kawakatsu characterized China in the Six Dynasties (and Sui-T'ang) as "medieval" (*chūsei*).[u] The medieval period had "overcome" the ancient period, and in turn it became the womb for the formation of modern China. Traditional Chinese society had not ceased with antiquity but had *progressed* to medieval and modern times by "overcoming" its own inner contradictions. Tanigawa and Kawakatsu both use the language of dialectical analysis but without the economic reductionism often characteristic of Marxist materialism. Thus, periodization—when the underlying principles of antiquity were "transcended" (*shiyō* or *chōkoku*)[v,w] by those of medieval times—becomes a central concern. This concern, however, is devoted less specifically to the dating of this transcendence than it is to those "underlying principles," the essential social fabric in ancient and medieval times.

The Marxists argued (and still argue) that these "principles," which unite everything from the individual peasants through the society to the state and its institutions, are the ascending phases of modes of production, as applicable in their universality to European as to non-European societies. For the reasons outlined earlier, Tanigawa and others sought to go beyond the labels of class and production mode and to locate the central elements that linked the people in local society. Tanigawa argued that it was "the historian's responsibility to capture the living universe (*sei no sekai*)[x] of the common people." To focus solely on production relations and systems of ownership, he claimed, ignored how people actually interacted in their day-to-day lives.[16]

The conceptual tool he developed was *kyōdōtai*[y] or "community," originally a Japanese neologism devised in the early twentieth century as a translation in the field of sociology for the German term *Gemeinde*.[17] The term *kyōdōtai* and theories concerning its application to virtually every society in the world abound.[18] Generally speaking, Japanese Marxists of a firm Weberian inclination (or Weberians with a Marxist predilection) have used the concept of *kyōdōtai* as a means of explaining those elements of social life that seemed to transcend class distinctions. For example, polder-watching was an activity of great importance to Chinese landlords and peasants alike, in that both relied on production from the land and could ill afford uncontrolled flooding. Thus, this activity was of a "communitarian" (*kyōdōtai teki*)[z] nature.

The uninitiated Western reader may be somewhat at a loss here, for most Western sociologists, philosophers, and historians (with the major exception of the Frankfurt School) have seen Marx and Weber as antagonistic opposites, as representative of entirely contrary points of view. Many Japanese scholars, however, with their unique capacity for bringing a variety of seemingly opposing strains together, did not pose Marx against Weber, but looked rather for ways they could complement each other.

The case of Ōtsuka Hisao, the foremost theoretician of *kyōdōtai* in Japan, is point in fact.[19] According to Ōtsuka, the "community" is not a classless, primitive, communal organization. Rather, at various stages of societal development, the "community" (the locus of subjective, everyday life and the bonds it creates between people) gives rise to class differentiation by its own internal necessity. It then changes its base and structure to support its class relations, a process that continues through the collapse of successive forms of production. Thus, classes emerge from the internal contradictions within the "community," and it is the unity, in class society, of these contradictions between private and public systems of ownership, between class and communal institutions, that comprises *kyōdōtai*. Modern capitalism tends to destroy *kyōdōtai*, according to Ōtsuka, although recent debate leaves this issue a theoretically open question.[20] There are also differences among Japanese historians and sociologists who employ the concept of *kyōdōtai* in their research concerning whether *kyōdōtai* really ameliorated class conflict or simply masked it.

Tanigawa and Kawakatsu have adopted this theory with modifications for the study of social relations in the Six Dynasties period in China. They argue that "communitarian" bonds remain more basic to the historical process, more logical, and ultimately more fundamental than classes over China's long-term social development. Following Ōtsuka's model, they show that principles of class different from those of *kyōdōtai* are born of the self-development of *kyōdōtai*, and that a specific historical "community" constitutes the unity of contradictory elements formed by these two opposing principles. Because *kyōdōtai* of necessity subsumes contradictions, it will develop of itself through history. Thus, they argue, *kyōdōtai* becomes the primary element for historical analysis.[21]

It is important to reiterate that Tanigawa and Kawakatsu do not deny the existence either of classes or of class conflict. *Kyōdōtai* in the hands of most postwar theorists assumes classes in society and looks in societies like China for the reasons the elite was able to prevent the explosion of conflict for such a long period. It looks, in other words, for the cohesive elements that bind potentially antagonistic classes or groups, for better or for worse, rather than the disruptive elements. Tanigawa goes a step further by relegating class tensions a secondary role to the primacy of the "communitarian" bonds between literati-aristocrats and commoners in the Six Dynasties period. To the Marxists, this is tantamount to denying the motive force in history, the most basic force for progress—class struggle. For this reason, which remains tacit, Tanigawa is often attacked by them as some sort of apostate.

Japanese Marxist historians regarded the entire period of Chinese history from Ch'in (and the inception of a unified empire) through T'ang as China's ancient age, because their sole criterion for historical demarcation was the system of ownership that demonstrated no significant change, they claimed, until the Sung introduced new forms of relations on the land. When we delve deep into the nature of social bonds, using *kyōdōtai* as a standard for analysis, Tanigawa argues, then the Ch'in-Han period immediately must be distinguished from the Sui-T'ang. The breakdown in the Spring and Autumn and Warring States eras of the clan (*shih-tsu*)[aa] *kyōdōtai* from the Shang-Chou period did not develop into a system of slavery. Rather, it led to a society of self-producing peasants who managed their families' lives on a local, small-scale basis. They formed relatively small population centers known as *li*[ab] or hamlets whose reasons for materializing concerned rituals, defense, cooperation in production, and the like. This corresponds to the "hamlet community" (or *ri kyōdōtai*[ac] in Tanigawa's phraseology). The leaders of the *li* were generally experienced, older men of local repute known as elders (*fu-lao*)[ad] who shared blood or fictive kin ties.

Over the four centuries of the Han dynasty's rule, though, a bifurcation within the local "community" developed between the large landowners (*hao-tsu*)[ae] who continued to amass ever-larger tracts of land and the increasingly large number of propertyless peasants who had lost their families' lands to *hao-tsu*. This development Tanigawa sees as the primary cause for the weakening of the public authority of the Han state, eventually bringing about its collapse. In the Six Dynasties that followed the disintegration of the Han, a new *kyōdōtai* emerged in local society. It featured an aristocracy of neither birth nor wealth, but rather one that owed its distinction to its cultured, intellectual quality, to its ability to rule in a human and humane way in times of serious strife, to its capacity to provide succor to the people in time of need, and (as Kawakatsu Yoshio put it) to its understanding of the need to restrain its own tendency toward limitless annexation of lands, a lesson from the Han experience. The new *kyōdōtai* thus embodied an ethic or a spirit of Confucian morality and Taoist selflessness in daily life. For these reasons, Tanigawa and Kawakatsu have argued that the fundamental distinction between the nature of the local "community" through the late Latter Han and that which developed in the Six Dynasties era deserves recognition as a basic point for periodizing Chinese history—from ancient to medieval times.[22]

It is this quality, the ethical-moral basis for the cohesion of the local community in the Six Dynasties, which has caused the most critical consternation over Tanigawa's application of *kyōdōtai* theory. Before we examine the debate over this issue, we should look a bit more closely at what this quality entails analytically as well as historiographically. As mentioned earlier, Tanigawa's reliance on *kyōdōtai* theory was born of a dissatisfaction with the highly influential Marxist "class conception of history" (*kaikyū shikan*)[af] that had risen to virtual sanctity among Japanese scholars. The intent was not to deny class relations in society, but to reach down to a more basic level and thus understand the specific role of class in medieval China.[23] Chinese society in the Six Dynasties period produced an aristocratic system with ranks of pedigree and all the associated trappings. But, Tanigawa argues, it did not develop the kind of territorial feudalism seen in Western Europe and Japan because of the nature of the bond between aristocrat and "commoner." Chinese aristocrats of this era were literati or men of letters (*wen-jen*)[ag] whose talents as such were respected in virtually every "dynastic" house of this long period of division. Despite nearly four centuries of military fighting and chaos, China never evolved the ethos for a military ruling class or a feudal military society. Because of the priority accorded these men of letters by state and local society alike, and because they were judged on the basis of their performance of their ethical creed in action, Chinese culture and civilization emerged from this long period advanced and enriched. Its sphere expanded beyond its own borders or, as Naitō Konan put it, Chinese history became the history of East Asia.[24]

There is something of surpassing import in this notion of "community" and the social bonds it fostered. The mechanistic manner in which class labels were attached by Japanese Marxists to various stages of Chinese social development obscured far more than it illuminated. In a critical summary of the *kyōdōtai* debate as applied to studies of the Six Dynasties period, one Japanese scholar cited the letter of an early eighteenth-century Jesuit missionary (admittedly at a much later time in Chinese history) who observed with profound incredulity how Chinese from neighboring villages managed to cooperate in times of trouble, such as when roads became impassable because of inclement weather, and to treat each other with respect and understanding, the exact opposite of what this man had often observed in Europe.[25] In short, *kyōdō-tai* in Tanigawa's usage bespeaks an effort to study Chinese society as the social relations of real human beings, not subsuming this concern to a standardized litany, but looking directly at what the available sources tell us in order to reconstruct the human element, which is of course the basis of society.

Many a non-Marxist scholar will find Tanigawa's assessment of the roles played by the "aristocracy" in the Six Dynasties period difficult to accept. One need not be a Marxist to be considerably less sanguine than Tanigawa in this regard. The reader of this volume will be struck by the author's apparent willingness to bend over backward to understand the aristocracy. And, in fact, Tanigawa's arguments do seem inordinately naive, particularly when he discusses the nature and composition of the Six Dynasties aristocracy and its relationship with the people. Several reasons can be suggested to explain this.

One should point first to Tanigawa's great irritation or anger with Marxist writings on Chinese history and particularly on the so-called "ancient" and "feudal" periods. He sees their imposition of models from abstract theory or political considerations onto the fabric of the development of Chinese society as inimical to understanding Chinese realities. In his view, they blur, obstruct, and ignore a great deal in their efforts to explain; and he shows parallels with American "modernization" theory in this area. In order to combat the dominance of Marxist historiography, he has purposefully overstated a non-Marxist argument that grants much to the consciousness and good will of a class the Marxists instinctively view as repressive. It is important to note this in advance, because the Western reader who comes to the debate midstream will surely find Tanigawa's views idealistic, unless something of the development of their background is known. Tanigawa also expects that his readers will not assume him to be a monarchist or an apologist for rule by an aristocracy, even a cultured one, or for that matter an idealist.

Part of the reason that one may find Tanigawa's argument naive also harks back to the earlier point that *kyōdōtai* theory assumes class conflict, and Tanigawa talks almost not at all about tensions between aristocrats and commoners but rather concentrates on how aristocrats sought to overcome conflict. Part of the problem, though, is simply that Tanigawa has overstated the case and does tend to present a rather rosy, perhaps idealistic, conception of aristocratic morality in the Six Dynasties period. As yet, his critics have all come from the Marxist camp. We await a non-Marxist critique to open the debate in a nondogmatic direction. Whatever the faults of his theory, Tanigawa has gone a long way toward overcoming the Marxist manner of applying preconceived colors and painting by the numbers in their work on this period.

The Kyōdōtai Debate

Tanigawa's reformulation of the central issues for studying Six Dynasties China led to a caustic exchange, what one author recently called "an unusually fierce debate in modern historiographical circles,"[26] often illuminating less than one might have hoped. Because of the vituperative and concomitant exaggerations by the participants, uninitiated readers may feel as though they have been dropped head first into a pit of vipers. The first respondent to take up the gauntlet against Tanigawa, Kawakatsu, and their allies raised an unfortunate issue at first that influenced much of the animosity in the subsequent exchange—Tanigawa's apostasy from Marxism. This critic was the accomplished Ming-Ch'ing social historian Shigeta Atsushi, and his views represented the position of the Rekishigaku kenkyūkai.

In 1969 Shigeta launched an unmitigated frontal assault on Tanigawa and Kawachi Jōzō[ah] for their calling the Six Dynasties period "feudal" (and medieval), rather than ancient, and by insinuation having strayed from the laws of historical materialism laid out by the Rekishigaku kenkyūkai. Shigeta clearly saw conversion (*tenkō*)[ai] to a non-Marxist methodology as condemnable in and of itself, scarcely needing empirical proof to the contrary of the new methodology. Particularly hard to stomach for Shigeta was how *kyōdōtai* was presented by Tanigawa and others for historical analysis. He saw Tanigawa's concept as suprahistorical, impossible to ground in the language of class, excessive in its emphasis on ethical-spiritual qualities, and ultimately just a matching assumed for the societal base that reflected the aristocratic system. In other words, he claimed that they looked at Six Dynasties society, saw an aristocratic superstructure, and posited a corresponding *kyōdōtai* substructure. This approach failed, Shigeta argued, because it ignored the truly important economic system at the base of society, which really was the substructure after all.[27]

There was another damning element in the Tanigawa thesis from Shigeta's perspective. Tanigawa's reperiodization of medieval Chinese history fit precisely with Naitō Konan's of two generations ago—Six Dynasties, Sui, and T'ang. Also, the stress on culture in Tanigawa's picture of the new aristocracy in this period struck a respondent note at the very heart of Naitō's conception of history, *bunkashi*[aj] or cultural history. It is well known and needs little explication in Japanese historical circles that Naitō was not a Marxist, did not analyze Chinese "feudalism," has been vilified by many Japanese Marxists as a prewar intellectual apologist for imperialism, and believed the development of culture to be the central process in historical development. Thus, from the Japanese Marxist perspective, it is sufficient to associate someone's name (in this case, Tanigawa's) with that of Naitō to establish guilt.[28]

One of the things that makes this debate interesting and particularly guiling for the critics of Tanigawa is that, despite obvious differences in their theories, Tanigawa will not disown Naitō; on the contrary, he writes in glowing terms of Naitō's remarkable vision concerning key issues in Chinese history, such as the dynamic element he sees in Naitō's view of historical development (by implication, a refutation of the idea that Naitō popularized a notion of "stagnant China"). He also explicitly claims to follow Naitō's periodization of the medieval period.[29]

Shigeta's attack was less scholarly than it was ideological, and it elicited several immediate responses from Tanigawa and Kawakatsu. In one coauthored essay, they sought to address Shigeta's critique by elaborating the importance of understanding medieval Chinese society in their way, the postwar intellectual milieu from which it emerged, and the significant elements of *kyōdōtai*.[30] Tanigawa then penned his own direct rebuttal to Shigeta in which he argued again that adherence to a fixed formula (*teishiki*)[ak] for historical development hindered our further understanding of Chinese historical realities. He agreed that he had once believed the Rekishigaku kenkyūkai line of ascending historical stages and their corresponding modes of production, but its failure to address crucial scholarly issues had led to reflection and eventually to criticism. Why, Tanigawa rhetorically wondered, was Shigeta harping on this apostasy and not on concrete scholarly problems?[31]

Kawakatsu pulled no punches in this regard. He compared Shigeta's overzealous concern with Tanigawa's change of views to the "trial of a heretic." Shigeta's continual attack on the notion of an aristocracy of culture drove Kawakatsu to the limit: "His [i.e., Shigeta's] astonishing ignorance of the history of scholarship on the Six Dynasties period and his attempt simply to employ categories only he himself trusts [i.e., categories of historical materialism] while discarding everything which fails to fit into this scheme derive from a bearing unbefitting a scholar."[32] Both Tanigawa and Kawakatsu also sought to defend their notions of the aristocracy, the "community," and the interaction of the two.

Shigeta's essay proved an unhappy first thrust at a Marxist rebuttal because it was so thoroughly tendentious. Later, though, more studied critiques of Tanigawa and Kawakatsu appeared in print; in fact, a flood of essays inundated the scholarly press in the early 1970s. Goi Naohiro, Tanaka Masatoshi, Hori Toshikazu, and a host of others all attacked Tanigawa's notion of *kyōdōtai* for the injustice they perceived it had done to class theory. All argued that class was more important than *kyōdōtai*. Tanaka alone did not dismiss Tanigawa's idea as the ravings of an illogical madman. He argued instead that what Tanigawa had identified as *kyōdōtai* was in fact an "ideological form," a "phenomenal form," or a "reflection of the superstructure." Before Tanaka could accept this notion, Tanigawa would have to elaborate in full materialist detail the essence of this *kyōdōtai*. When he reviewed the debate in 1974, Tanigawa noted that although he did not agree with Tanaka, at least he felt Tanaka understood what he was trying to do with *kyōdōtai* theory and Six Dynasties history, which Shigeta had not.[33]

One criticism raised by a number of scholars was the lack of precision in Tanigawa's defining of *kyōdōtai*. Tanigawa agreed that this was a task still being worked out, but that did not preclude its use as a sociological tool in historical analysis. By using this sociological term to help uncover and explain historical facts, its methodological structure would become more refined. An even more prominent criticism of *kyōdōtai*, which even Shigeta had noted, was that Tanigawa and Kawakatsu had overplayed the ethical or spiritual element at work in "community" dynamics. It must be understood that positing the "ethical" or the "spiritual" as historically significant is anathema to hard-line Marxist critics or, at best, is considered by less dogmatic Marxists to be mistaking a reflection of reality for reality itself. However, the crux of the matter for either group, and the large area in between them, is that nothing can be more important than class in history.[34] If *kyōdōtai* were made secondary to the role of class in history, no one would have any theoretical problems with it, but Tanigawa and Kawakatsu have argued for its primacy in premodern Chinese history. For that reason, and particularly since Tanigawa once counted himself within the historical materialist fold, they have received a virtual barrage of criticism.

Although the volume translated here was not specifically meant to address the outpouring of criticism, it effectively did just that by reviewing not the history of *kyōdōtai* debate but the issues involved in the study of "medieval China." This task necessitated a reinvestigation of the major schools of thought regarding Chinese "feudalism" and the dating of China's "medieval age." It also allowed Tanigawa to describe more fully how *kyōdōtai* might best be understood in the concrete realities of the Six Dynasties period. The book divides into these two major sections.[35]

Kawakatsu has long maintained an association with French sinologists and in fact spent a period of time studying in France. Two of his essays have appeared in French, the most recent being a brief explanation of his and Tanigawa's conception of Six Dynasties history. A German analysis of Tanigawa's notion of *kyōdōtai* for the study of medieval China was published several years ago. Recently, a balanced exposition of Tanigawa's (and the "Kyoto school's") analysis of the place of the "medieval era" in Chinese history appeared in the foremost journal of Soviet Asian studies. It was almost immediately translated (for internal consumption only, *nei-pu fa-hsing*)[al] in the People's Republic of China. Furthermore, the theories of Tanigawa and Kawakatsu figure significantly in a recent study of postwar Japanese sinology to emerge from Taiwan.[36] The publication of this volume of Tanigawa's marks the first serious discussion of his work in English[37] and the first translation into English of any of his writings. It is hoped that the issues raised here will provide food for thought not only for "medievalists" but also for students of other eras in Chinese history.

Glossary

Notes

(All publishers are located in Tokyo unless otherwise noted.)

1. Niida Noboru仁井田陞, "Chūgoku shakai no 'hōken' to fyūdarizumu" 中国社会の封建とフューダリズム (*Feng-chien* and feudalism in Chinese society), in Niida, *Chūgoku hōsei shi kenkyū* 中国法制史研究 (Studies in Chinese legal history), vol. 3, *Dorei nōdo hō, kazoku sonraku hō* 奴隸農奴法・家族村落法 (Laws governing slavery and serfdom, laws governing the family and the village), Tokyo University Press, 1962, pp. 97–100.

2. This view has recently been reiterated in a Chinese essay on the subject: Yu Hsin-ch'un 俞辛焞, "Shih-lun Jih-pen te chan-hou kai-ko (shang)" 試論日本的戰后改革(上) (A study of Japan's postwar reforms, part 1), *Shih-chieh li-shih* 世界歷史 5 (1980), pp. 12–14.

3. See, for example, the following works: Kuwabara Takeo桑原武夫, ed., *Burujowa kakumei no hikaku kenkyū* ブルジョワ革命の比較研究 (Comparative studies in bourgeois revolutions), Chikuma shobō, 1964; Kobayashi Yoshiaki 小林良彰, *Meiji ishin no kangaekata*明治維新の考之方 (A way of thinking about the Meiji Restoration), San'ichi shobō, 1967, esp. part 2 entitled "Meiji ishin to Furansu kakumei wa onaji mono ka" 明治維新とフランス革命は同じものか (Were the Meiji Restoration and the French Revolution the same thing?), pp. 115–247; Kobayashi Yoshiaki, *Furansu kakumei shi nyūmon* フランス革命史入門 (Introduction to the history of the French Revolution), San'ichi shobō, 1978; and Inoue Kōji 井上幸治, *Kindai shizō no mosaku: Furansu kakumei to Chichibu jiken* 近代史像の模索：フランス革命と秩父事件 (In search of a view of modern history: The French Revolution and the Chichibu Incident), Byakushobō, 1976.

4. Frederico Chabod, *Storia dell'idea d'Europa* (History of the idea of Europe), Rome, 1959; translated into Japanese by Shimizu Jun'ichi 清水純一, *Yōroppa no imi* ヨーロッパの意味 (The meaning of Europe), Saimaru shuppansha, 1969, pp. 23–24 and esp. chapter 4.

5. For Nishijima's essay claiming slavery as the basis of Ch'in-Han society, Masubuchi's critique, and Nishijima's published retreat, see Tanigawa's treatment of the whole issue in this volume.

6. Tanigawa Michio 谷川道雄, "Ichi Tōyōshi kenkyūsha ni okeru genjitsu to gakumon" 一東洋史研究者における現実と学問 (Reality and scholarship for one scholar of East Asian history), *Atarashii rekishigaku no tame ni* 新しい歴史学のために 68 (1961), reprinted in Tanigawa, *Chūgoku chūsei shakai to kyōdotai* 中国中世社会と共同体 (Medieval Chinese society and "community"), Kokusho kankōkai, 1976, pp. 119–135; Tanigawa, "Chūgoku shi kenkyū no atarashii kadai sairon: Shigeta Atsushi-shi 'Hōkensei no shiten to Min-Shin shakai' o yonde" 中国史研究の新らしい課題再論：重田徳氏「封建制の視點と明清社会」を読んで (Another look at a new theme in the study of Chinese history: On reading Mr. Shigeta Atsushi's "The standpoint of feudalism and Ming-Ch'ing society"), *Tōyōshi kenkyū* 東洋史研究 28.2–3 (December 1969), pp. 111–112; and Tanigawa, "Gi-Shin-Nambokuchō" 魏晋

南北朝 (Wei, Chin, Northern and Southern Dynasties), *Shigaku zasshi* 史学雑誌 71.5 (May 1962), pp. 164–171; and *Shigaku zasshi* 76.5 (May 1967), pp. 201–207.

7. Tanigawa, *Zui-Tō teikoku keisei shiron* 隋唐帝国形成史論 (A historical analysis of the formation of the Sui-T'ang empire), Chikuma shobō, 1971, pp. 5–7.

8. We now have such studies as: David Johnson, *The Chinese Medieval Oligarchy*, Boulder, Colo., Westview Press, 1977; Patricia Ebrey, *The Aristocratic Families of Early Imperial China: A Case Study of the Po-ling Ts'ui Family*, Cambridge, Cambridge University Press, 1978; and a forthcoming conference volume, *The Nature of State and Society in Early Medieval China*. We also have translations of important texts of the period, such as *Pao-p'u-tzu, Yen-shih chiahsün*, and *Wen-hsüan* (in process).

9. Kawakatsu Yoshio 川勝義雄, *Gi-Shin-Nambokuchō: Sōdai na bunretsu jidai* 魏晋南北朝：壮大な分裂時代 (Wei, Chin, Northern and Southern dynasties: An era of great disunity), Kōdansha, 1974, p. 268.

10. The major study to note here is Miyazaki Ichisada 宮崎市定, *Kyūhin kanjin hō no kenkyū: Kakyo zenshi* 九品官人法の研究：科挙前史 (A study of the laws concerning officials in the Nine Ranks system: A prehistory to the examination system), Kyoto, Tōyōshi kenkyūkai, 1956. See also David Johnson, op. cit., pp. 20–26; Yang Yün-ju 楊筠如, *Chiu-p'in chung-cheng yü Liuch'ao men-fa* 九品中正與六朝門閥 (The Nine Ranks and Arbiter system and aristocratic cliques in the Six Dynasties period), Shanghai, Commercial Press, 1930; and Donald Holtzman, "Les débuts du système médiéval de choix et de classement des fonctionnaires: Les Neuf Catégories et l'Impartial et Juste," in *Mélanges publiés par l'Institut des Hautes Études Chinoises*, vol. 1 (Bibliotèque de l'Institut des Hautes Études Chinoises, Vol. XI), Paris, Presses universitaires de France, 1957, pp. 387–414.

11. On Naitō Konan, see Joshua Fogel, *Politics and Sinology: The Case of Naitō Konan (1866–1934)*, Cambridge, Mass., Council on East Asian Studies, Harvard University, 1984.

12. 概括的唐宋時代観, *Rekishi to chiri* 歴史と地理 9.5 (May 1922). This essay is reprinted in Naitō's collected works, *Naitō Konan zenshū* 内藤湖南全集, Chikuma shobō, 1969–1976, Vol. VIII, pp. 111–119. It is translated in Joshua Fogel, *Naitō Konan and the Development of the Conception of "Modernity" in Chinese History*, Armonk, N.Y., M. E. Sharpe, Publishers, 1984, pp. 88–99.

13. See Naitō's *Shina jōko shi* 支那上古史 (Ancient Chinese history) and his *Shina chūko no bunka* 支那中古の文化 (Medieval Chinese culture), both in *Naitō Konan zenshū*, Vol. X. Naitō often cited as his authority on the aristocracy in this period the eighteenth-century Chinese historian Chao I 趙翼.

14. A sampling of these three men's work would have to include: Okazaki Fumio 岡崎文夫, *Gi-Shin-Nambokuchō tsūshi* 魏晋南北朝通史 (Comprehensive history of the Wei, Chin, and Northern and Southern dynasties), Kyoto, Kōbundō, 1932; Okazaki, *Nambokuchō ni okeru shakai keizai seido* 南北朝における社会経済制度 (Social and economic institutions in the Northern and Southern dynasties), Kōbundō, 1935; Okazaki and Ikeda Shizuo 池田静夫, *Kōnan bunka kaihatsu shi: Sono chiri teki kiso kenkyū* 江南文化開發史：その地理的基礎研究 (The history of the expansion of culture in Kiangnan: A study of its geographical foundations), Kōbundō, 1940; Miyakawa Hisayuki 宮川尚志, *Shokatsu Kōmei* 諸葛孔明 (Chu-ko K'ungming), Shina rekishi chiri sōsho, 1940; Miyakawa, *Rikuchō shi kenkyū, seiji*

shakai hen 六朝史研究, 政治社会篇 (Studies in Six Dynasties history, volume on political and social problems), Nihon gakujutsu shinkōkai, 1956; Miyakawa, *Rikuchō shi kenkyū, shūkyō hen* 六朝史研究, 宗教篇 (Studies in Six Dynasties history, volume on religious problems), Heirakuji shoten, 1964; Miyakawa, *Shokatsu Kōmei: Sangoku shi to sono jidai* 諸葛孔明:「三国志」とその時代 (Chu-ko K'ung-ming: The *San-kuo chih* and its age), Sōgensha, 1966; Utsunomiya Kiyoyoshi 宇都宮清吉, *Kandai shakai keizai shi kenkyū* 漢代社会経済史研究 (Studies in the social and economic history of the Han dynasty), Kōbundō, 1955; Utsunomiya and Masumura Hiroshi 増村宏, translators, *Gi-Shin-Nambokuchō keizai shi* 魏晋南北朝経済史 (An economic history of the Wei, Chin, and Northern and Southern dynasties), by Wu Hsien-ch'ing 武仙卿, Seikatsusha, 1942; Utsunomiya, *Chūgoku kodai chūsei shi kenkyū* 中国古代中世研究 (Studies in ancient and medieval Chinese history), Sōbunsha, 1977. For the Miyakawa essay on Naitō Konan, see "An Outline of the Naitō Hypothesis and Its Effects on Japanese Studies of China," *Far Eastern Quarterly* 14.4 (August 1955), pp. 533–553.

15. Naitō's most famous disciple, Miyazaki Ichisada, later revised the master's periodization to include a "most modern" (*sai kinsei* 最近世) era dating from the 1911 Revolution. He retained Naitō's cultural historical approach while reassessing the importance of events in the twentieth century. See his *Chūgoku shi* 中国史 (History of China), Iwanami shoten, 1977, vol. 1, pp. 13–14, 35–36, 82–86. The first forthright critique of Naitō along these lines was Nohara Shirō 野原四郎, "Naitō Konan *Shinaron* hihan" 内藤湖南支那論批判 (A critique of Naitō Konan's *Shinaron*), *Chūgoku hyōron* 中国評論 1.4 (1946), pp. 35–42.

16. Tanigawa, "'Kyōdōtai' ronsō ni tsuite: Chūgoku shi kenkyū ni okeru shisō jōkyō" 「共同体」論争について:中国史研究における思想状況 (On the debate over *kyōdōtai*: The intellectual state of Chinese historical studies), *Nagoya jimbun kagaku kenkyūkai nempō* 名古屋人文科学研究会年報 1(1974), pp. 71–72.

17. Whenever the terms "community" or "communitarian" appear in quotation marks, they are meant as translations of the Japanese term *kyōdōtai*.

18. For an introduction to *kyōdōtai* theory as applied to Chinese society, see Hatada Takashi 旗田巍, "Chūgoku ni okeru sensei shugi to 'sonraku kyōdōtai riron'" 中国における専制主義と「村落共同体理論」(Despotism in China and the "theory of the village community"), *Chūgoku kenkyū* 中国研究 13 (September 1950), pp. 2–12; reprinted in Hatada, *Chūgoku sonraku to kyōdōtai riron* 中国村落と共同体理論 (The Chinese village and *kyōdōtai* theory), Iwanami shoten, 1976, pp. 3–19; and Imahori Seiji 今堀誠二, "Sonraku kyōdōtai" 村落共同体 (The village "community"), in *Ajia rekishi jiten* アジア歴史事典 (Encyclopedia of Asian history), Heibonsha, 1960, vol. 5, pp. 413–417.

19. See Takeshi Ishida, "A Current Japanese Interpretation of Max Weber," *The Developing Economies* IV.3 (September 1966), pp. 349–366; and Hisao Ōtsuka, "Max Weber's View of Asian Society, with Special Reference to His Theory of the Traditional Community," *The Developing Economies* IV.3 (September 1966), pp. 275–298.

20. Ōtsuka Hisao 大塚久雄, *Kyōdōtai no kiso riron* 共同体の基礎理論 (The basic theory of *kyōdōtai*, 1955), reprinted in *Ōtsuka Hisao chosakushū* 大塚久雄著作集 (The writings of Ōtsuka Hisao), Iwanami shoten, 1971, vol. 7, pp. 6–8; and Ōtsuka, "Kyodōtai kaitai no kiso teki shojōken, sono riron

teki kōsatsu" 共同体解体の基礎的諸条件：その理論的考察(The basic conditions for the dissolution of *kyōdōtai*: A theoretical investigation, 1962), in *Ōtsuka Hisao chosakushū*, vol. 7, pp. 107–133.

21. Kawakatsu Yoshio and Tanigawa Michio, "Chūgoku chūsei shi kenkyū ni okeru tachiba to hōhō" 中国中世史研究における立場と方法 (Standpoint and method in the study of medieval Chinese history), in *Chūgoku chūsei shi kenkyū: Rikuchō Zui-Tō no shakai to bunka* 中国中世史研究：六朝隋唐の社会と文化 (Studies in medieval Chinese history: Society and culture in the Six Dynasties, Sui, and T'ang), edited by Chūgoku chūsei shi kenkyūkai 中国中世史研究会, Tōkai University Press, 1970, pp. 10–12.

22. Summarized in Tanigawa, "'Kyōdōtai' ronsō," pp. 72–74, 79, 81; and Tanigawa, "Chūgoku shi kenkyū no," p. 119. Discussed at length in the Tanigawa text here translated as well as in Kawakatsu, *Gi-Shin-Nambokuchō*.

23. Tanigawa, "'Kyōdōtai' ronsō," pp. 81, 89.

24. Naitō Konan, *Shina jōko shi*, in *Naitō Konan zenshū*, Vol. X, p. 11. See also Kawakatsu, *Gi-Shin-Nambokuchō*, pp. 71, 74, 380–382; and Kawakatsu, "L'aristocratie et la société féodale au début des Six Dynasties," *Zimbun* 17 (1981), p. 160.

25. Satake Yasuhiko 佐竹靖彦, "Chūgoku zenkindai shi ni okeru kyōdōtai to kyōdōtai ron ni tsuite no oboegaki: Tanigawa Michio-shi no kenkai o tegakari ni" 中国前近代史における共同体と共同体論についての覚え書：谷川道雄氏の見解を手がかりに (Notes on *kyōdōtai* and the debate over *kyōdōtai* in premodern Chinese history: Mr. Tanigawa Michio's views), *Jimbun gakuhō* 人文学報 154 (1982), p. 84.

26. Satake, p. 85.

27. Shigeta Atsushi 重田徳, "Hōkensei no shiten to Min-Shin shakai" 封建制の視點と明清社会 (The standpoint of feudalism and Ming-Ch'ing society), *Tōyōshi kenkyū* 27.4 (March 1969), pp. 164–165, 175, 179; and Kawakatsu Yoshio, "Shigeta-shi no Rikuchō hōkensei ron hihan ni tsuite" 重田氏の六朝封建制論批判について (On Mr. Shigeta's critique of the view of the Six Dynasties era as feudal), *Rekishi hyōron* 歴史評論 247 (February 1971), pp. 58, 61–62, 64.

28. See Shigeta's continued attack in "Chūgoku hōkensei kenkyū no hōkō to hōhō: Rikuchō hōkensei ron no ichi kensatsu" 中国封建制研究の方向と方法：六朝封建論の一検察 (Directions and methods in the study of Chinese feudalism: An investigation of the theory of feudalism in the Six Dynasties period), *Rekishi hyōron* 247 (February 1971), esp. pp. 45–47.

29. Tanigawa, *Sekai teikoku no keisei* 世界帝国の形成 (The formation of a world empire), Kōdansha gendai shinsho, 1977, pp. 8–9. See also Kawakatsu, "L'aristocratie," p. 107.

30. Kawakatsu and Tanigawa, "Chūgoku chūsei shi," pp. 3–13.

31. Tanigawa, "Chūgoku shi kenkyū no," pp. 109–117.

32. Kawakatsu, "Shigeta-shi no," pp. 61–69, quotation on p. 63.

33. Goi Naohiro 五井直弘, "Chūgoku kodai shi to kyōdōtai: Tanigawa Michio-shi no shoron o megutte" 中国古代史と共同体：谷川道雄氏の所論をめぐって (Ancient Chinese history and *kyōdōtai*: On Mr. Tanigawa Michio's argument), *Rekishi hyōron* 255 (October 1971), pp. 87–99; and Tanaka Masatoshi 田中正俊, "Chūgoku no henkaku to hōkensei kenkyū no kadai (1)" 中国の変革と封建制研究の課題 (The transformation of China and tasks in the study of feudalism, part 1), *Rekishi hyōron* 271 (December 1972), esp. pp. 52–57. Two critical reviews of the volumes of essays on medieval Chinese history introduced by Tanigawa and Kawakatsu (cited in note 21) are: Hori Toshikazu 堀敏一, in *Shigaku zasshi* 80.2 (February 1971), pp. 77–87;

and Otagi Hajime 愛宕元, in *Shirin* 史林 53.6 (November 1970), pp. 156–161. In the annual survey of historical literature published each May in *Shigaku zasshi*, this book of essays warranted consideration in three separate sections: Fukui Shigemasa 福井重雅, "Sengoku Shin-Kan" 戦国秦漢 (Warring States, Ch'in, Han); Kikuchi Hideo 菊地英夫, "Gi-Shin-Nambokuchō" 魏晋南北朝 (Wei, Chin, Northern and Southern dynasties); Kurihara Masao 栗原益男, "Zui-Tō" 隋唐 (Sui, T'ang), all in *Shigaku zasshi* 80.5 (May 1971), pp. 187–188, 189–197, and 198–203, respectively. For Tanigawa's response to all of this, see Tanigawa, "'Kyōdōtai' ronsō," pp. 66–67, 76, 82–83.

34. Kimata Norio 木全徳雄, "Chūgoku kodai chūsei shi ha'aku no shikaku to hōhō o megutte" 中国古代中世史把握の視角と方法をめぐって (On viewpoint and method for an understanding of ancient and medieval Chinese history), in *Suzuki hakushi koki kinen Tōyōgaku ronsō* 鈴木博士古稀記念東洋学論叢 (Symposium on East Asian studies in commemoration of the seventieth birthday of Professor Suzuki [Shun 俊]), Meitoku shuppansha, 1972, pp. 165–190; Fujiie Reinosuke 藤家礼之助, "Chūgoku kodai chūsei shakai no kōsatsu, bunki mondai shiron" 中国古代中世社会の考察：分期問題試論 (An investigation of ancient and medieval Chinese society, and a tentative analysis of the periodization issue), in *Rekishi ni okeru bummei no shosō: Tōkai daigaku sanjū shūnen kinen ronbunshū* 歴史における文明の諸相：東海大学三十周年記念論文集 (The various faces of civilization in history: Essays commemorating the thirtieth anniversary of Tōkai University), edited by Shōju Keitarō 尚樹啓太郎, Tōkai University Press, 1974, pp. 75–109; Hori Toshikazu, "Chūgoku kodai shi to kyōdōtai no mondai" 中国古代史と共同体の問題 (Ancient Chinese history and the issue of "community"), *Sundai shigaku* 駿台史学 27 (September 1970), pp. 162–183, reprinted in *Gendai rekishigaku no kadai (jō)* 現代の歴史学の課題（上）(Problems of contemporary historiography, part 1), Aoki shoten, 1971; Tada Kensuke 多田狷介, "Chūgoku kodai shi kenkyū oboegaki" 中国古代史研究覚書 (Notes on the study of medieval Chinese history), *Shisō* 史艸 12 (1971), pp. 1–45; and Ihara Kōsuke 伊原弘介, "Hōkensei no bunseki shiten to kaikyū shiten, kaikyū shiten o aimai ni suru futatsu no hōhō no hihan" 封建制の分析視点と階級視点：階級視点をあいまいにする二つの方法の批判 (Analyses of feudalism and the class standpoint, a critique of two methods that obscure the class standpoint), *Shigaku kenkyū* 史学研究 119 (August 1973), pp. 77–90. For Tanigawa's response, see his "'Kyōdōtai' ronso," pp. 78–80, 86–88.

35. The original of the translated text is: *Chūgoku chūsei shakai ron josetsu* 中国中世社会論序説 (An introduction to a theory of medieval Chinese society), in *Chūgoku chūsei shakai to kyōdōtai*, pp. 1–116.

36. Kawakatsu Yoshio, "La décadence de l'aristocratie chinoise sous les Dynasties du Sud," *Acta Asiatica* 21 (1971), pp. 13–38; and Kawakatsu, "L'aristocratie," pp. 107–160; Doris Heyde, "Haozu und dörfliche Gemeinde in China von 3 bis 6 Jahrhundert. Zu Tanigawa Michios Theorie von der Kommune in China," *Altorientalische Forschungen* IV (1976), pp. 327–337; V.V. Maliavin, "Kiotaskaia shkola i problema 'Srednykh vekov' v istorii Kitaia," *Narodi Azii i Afriki* 2 (1981), pp. 188–203; V.V. Ma-liang-wen 馬良文 [V.V. Maliavin], "Ching-tu hsüeh-p'ai ho Chung-kuo li-shih shang te 'Chung-shih-chi' wen-t'i" 京都学派和中国歴史上的「中世紀」問題 (The Kyoto school and the problem of the "medieval period" in Chinese history), *Chung-kuo shih yen-chiu tung-t'ai* 中国史研究動態 34 (October 1981), pp. 10–28; and Kao Ming-shih 高明士, *Chan-hou Jih-pen te Chung-kuo shih yen-chiu* 戰後日本的中国史研究 (Postwar Japanese studies of Chinese history),

Taipei, Tung-sheng ch'u-pan shih-yeh yu-hsien kung-ssu, 1982, pp. 60–61, 80–83.

37. Dennis Grafflin touches briefly on Tanigawa's and Kawakatsu's work, though not so much on the theoretical issues. See Grafflin, "The Great Family in Medieval South China," *Harvard Journal of Asiatic Studies* 41.1 (June 1981), pp. 65–74.

Preface to the English Edition

One of the concerns Europeans have held since the eighteenth century regarding the universe of the peoples of Asia has been to demonstrate in comparison to the European world whether human freedom existed in Asia. This concern was fitting to that universal age never witnessed before—modernity—when human society had been perfected. Numerous inquiries into China's past and present were born of this concern, and these studies exerted a powerful influence upon the intellectual worlds of both China and Japan. What would the future bring China, having just ended over two thousand years of despotism in the early twentieth century? What was the chance that her past and present prepared her for it? These sorts of issues were acutely felt by the Chinese themselves, as well as by the Japanese who were intimately involved as China's neighbors.

The image of traditional China held by many people became one of an age-old, despotic, bureaucratic state and a firm family system, with uniform village "communities." Confucian morality was said to embellish these institutions with an ideology, and together they crushed the Chinese people's spirit of freedom and impeded her historical progress toward becoming a free nation. When we look back at the extraordinary obstacles on China's path to modernity, we can sense in this negative view a part of the truth.

It is undeniable, though, that Chinese history pursued its own active development. We also must recognize the fact that the world has always held in highest esteem the unprecedented levels attained by traditional Chinese culture. In particular, the deep humanitarian spirit of Chinese thought and Chinese art has profoundly moved the minds of contemporary men. This fact seems widely divergent from, even opposed to, the view of the Chinese as slaves of despotism.

For the Japanese, this dilemma was virtually an ethnic one. Japanese culture had taken shape as Chinese culture spread to the ethnic groups living around China's borders. It proved extremely difficult, even meaningless, to differentiate what part of Japanese culture belonged originally to China and what part was native to the islands of Japan, as Chinese culture penetrated to the very body of the Japanese people. Thus, the Japanese longing for Chinese culture emerged from the roots of their own ethnic history.

For the Japanese people, who attained modernization so rapidly, however, contemporary China remained irrevocably a backward nation. The difference between the two nations in their speed of modernization buoyed the Japanese sense of superiority and, sadly, supported Japan's invasion of China. With the conclusion of World War II, one group of Japanese historians began a severe reflection of this whole issue, endeavoring to replace the stagnationist view of Chinese history with a developmental conception. Their attempt did not succeed, however, because they tried to apply general laws to Chinese history on the basis of the historical materialist formula (slavery–feudalism–capitalism), and as a result numerous facts were forced out of consideration so as to fit China into the preconceived mold. Thus, Chinese history was once again transformed into a history lacking a freedom of its own.

I have written a number of essays in an attempt to resolve this whole problem, and I have striven to describe an image of historical development within a structure inherent in Chinese history. My research has been nurtured in joint work with the two well-known scholars of medieval Chinese history, Utsunomiya Kiyoyoshi and Kawakatsu Yoshio, as well as others. My theories have given rise to a good number of debates in Japanese academic circles, which continue today.

As I have noted, the problem of human freedom in Chinese society is *the* important task with which contemporary historiography must wrestle. In other words, we must not limit the problem of human freedom to the European world or to modern society, but we must understand it from the manifold perspective of the human existence of the peoples of the world from the past through the present. The general outlines of my ideas are described in my book *Chūgoku chūsei shakai to kyōdō-*

tai (Medieval Chinese society and "community," 1976), and the most comprehensive section of this book has now been translated into English by Professor Joshua A. Fogel of Harvard University, who possesses both profound erudition in Chinese history as well as a remarkable grasp of the Japanese language. My work fundamentally relies on the theories of modern Japan's greatest scholar of China, Naitō Konan (1866–1934). That Professor Fogel is himself a scholar of Naitō Konan renders this translation of higher quality. I am deeply grateful to him for this work, and I sincerely hope that my views will elicit a frank response among the wider academic community.

Kyoto, Japan   Tanigawa Michio
June 1983

PART I

Chinese Society and Feudalism: An Investigation of the Past Literature

One

Introduction

Did Chinese society in fact experience an era that can be called feudal? If it did, which period was that and what form did it take? If it did not, then what sort of logical development has Chinese history as a whole pursued? The basic task of this part of the book is to disentangle this issue. My original intent was to come to terms with the unique nature of Chinese society by further investigating Chinese society from this perspective. Since I have been unable as yet to reach that goal, my present objective is a preparatory investigation to that end.

Why, then, must we ask if feudalism existed in China? To people for whom it is self-evident that Chinese society, like Western society, followed a course from ancient slavery to medieval feudalism to modern capitalism, or should have taken such a course, it may indeed seem strange to pose the question of the existence in Chinese history of feudalism. Yet, we are certainly not lacking for theories that deny the existence of feudalism in Chinese history. The two positions, affirming or denying feudalism, have a rather long history of debate themselves. This issue is actually linked directly to the issue of China's modernization.

Generally speaking, theses that affirm or deny feudalism have tended to bifurcate into diametrically opposed views with respect to the progressive nature of Chinese society. Those who believe China experienced feudalism argue that Chinese society basically followed a path of historical progress consistent with that of Western society. Those who deny feudalism argue that Chinese society was extraordinarily saturated with stagnancy, as compared to the West, and they assume that it existed in a qualitatively different historical world from Western society. In other words, the former conceive of a unilinear, monistic

3

world history, whereas the latter conceive of a two-tracked or multitracked world history.

These two points of view, though diametrically opposed, nonetheless share one aspect in common. Be it progress or stagnation, in either case the observation is rooted in modern Western society. In comparing it to the modern West (and its prehistory), they see Chinese society as either progressing or stagnating—merely different perspectives from the same line of vision. In this line of vision, it seems that the "modern West" is deeply tied up with a guiding conception for world history. Casting the least doubt on all this necessitates a basic reanalysis of both theories, progress and stagnation.

In the past, the issue that East Asian historical studies have confronted most revealingly has been the nature of the link between the societies of East Asia and of the modern world (with the West at the forefront) as an overall, continual process from ancient through modern times. It was here that the two opposing points of view were born, though neither side doubted that Chinese society would dissolve into the stream of the modern world. In this "modernization process," they wanted to see the evolution of the Chinese into ordinary people. However, we have reached a critical stage in which various negative factors in contemporary human existence have forced us to reexamine the significance of such a modernization process itself. The more modernization proceeds, the more people lose confidence in their existence as individual beings. This contradiction has consistently covered the contemporary world. This human crisis we see today must be linked to the nature of East Asian historical studies itself. The question, can East Asian historical studies maintain its integrity as a human science, seems to pose a tremendous hindrance to the development of our own field of research, which is only natural.

Now, however, there seems to be no more room for doubt that these preconceptions, which past scholars of East Asia took for granted, are themselves being undermined. We can no longer understand the realities of Chinese society in the context of world history solely within a framework of progress or stagnation. Where shall we find a new line of vision for our understanding of China? This book attempts to look along an untraveled path from the vantage point of an investigation of past scholarship into this problem of the existence or non-existence of a Chinese feudalism.

Two

Chinese Historical Studies in the Postwar Period and the Development of Conceptions of Feudalism

The Two Paths to Feudalism

One of the goals set by Japanese studies of Chinese history in the postwar period has been "to overcome the theory of stagnation." The defeat of Japanese imperialism in the war had the effect of thoroughly dismantling the Japanese people's sense of superiority with respect to China. The subsequent victory of the Chinese revolution was seen as factual proof of the fallacy of the theory of stagnation, which had been propounded even from within the Marxist camp. Thus, the problem became one of how to understand in a consistent manner the progressive nature of Chinese society from antiquity through modernity. The investigation of this problem was advanced on the basis of a belief in a rational scientific comprehension of history. Antithetical to the wartime ultranationalist conception of history, historical materialism as a method gained general currency. Max Weber's methodology also offered a powerful stimulus to the academic world.

Between the war and the postwar period, however, there was a large gap in historical research. Studies in history did not immediately develop in response to the new social conditions following the war. The scholarly world was utterly despondent, and the publication of Ishimoda Shō's painstaking work, *Chūsei teki sekai no keisei* (The formation of the medieval

5

world)[1] played a great role in filling this gap. This book was the result of wartime research by the author, himself a Marxist. It vividly and substantively described the historical process by which the temple-owned estates of ancient Japan grew through class conflicts over a long period of time into rule by medieval fiefdoms. In other words, Ishimoda attempted to demonstrate in concrete terms the transformation from the ancient slave system to medieval feudalism in Japan, a process characterized by the generation and growth of a system of domination by medieval territorial lords.

The ancient slave system spoken of here differs from the prototypical slavery that flourished in the classical ancient world. It was what might be called an Asiatic slavery in that it was strictly regulated under the *ritsuryō* system.[2] In its emergence, Japanese patriarchal-familial slavery displayed the same origins as the typical slave system while simultaneously preventing its further development. As a result one finds at that time the existence of a wide body of self-sustaining peasants. In this regard, the ancient Japanese imperial system was in many instances characterizable as feudal. The research of Watanabe Yoshimichi prior to the war, however, argued for a Japanese variety of slavery (or rather, more generally, an Asiatic slavery).[3] Ishimoda, who was a member of Watanabe's study group, traced the process through which a feudal-serf system was formed, using the thesis of a Japanese style of slavery.

The homeland of the *ritsuryō* system (this Japanese brand of slavery) was, needless to say, China in the era of the Sui-T'ang empire. Thus the emergence of a feudal domain system in Japan involved a process whereby Japan broke away from the ancient world in East Asia and forged her own distinctive path. This meant that Japan and China would subsequently diverge and proceed along different routes. In medieval China, social relations did not give rise to a system of territorial domains or to bands of warriors, as in Japan.

In 1939 the late Katō Shigeshi analyzed the historical differences between China and Japan. He argued that whereas in Japan a feudal system remained in existence over a long period of time, China had only experienced it early on in the Chou dynasty and that thereafter civil officials in a state bureaucracy had become the basis of Chinese government.

Katō's argument goes as follows. The Six Dynasties and late T'ang eras witnessed for a time the growth of private armies and the energetic activities of military men, but we do not see the development of a warrior class based on hereditary, lord-vassal relations, as in Japan. In China they were swallowed up into a civil government where power was centralized. The expression *pu-ch'ü*[a] had originally meant an army, but by the Sui-T'ang period it was a way of referring to the outcasts of society; this would indicate that military hierarchical relations did not mature into feudal hierarchical relations. Furthermore, this difference prescribed the nature of the social development of the Chinese and Japanese peoples, so that the evolution of a sound superior-inferior (lord-vassal, ruler-ruled) ethic in Japan nurtured the distinctive nature of the Japanese—profound in human emotions and firm in moral principles. It formed the basis for the sound development of the Japanese people.[4]

This observation by Katō offered a pioneering foreshadowing of the problem of the relationship between feudalism and modernization, to be discussed in a later section. What circumstances gave rise to this divergence between the Japanese system of warrior feudal domains and China's bureaucratic rule by civil government? Katō did not address this issue, but it is dealt with in Ishimoda's book.

Ishimoda found the reason for this difference in the nature of Chinese clan and in the differentiation of classes within the "village community" (*sonraku kyōdōtai* or *kyōdōtai*).[b,c] In China, class distinctions developed within the "community," giving rise to the opposition between landlord and tenant farmer, rich peasant and poor peasant. Yet China was characterized by the fact that while "community" relations worked well, they caused a blurring of class relations. For instance, organs of mutual aid within a single-clan village—such as relief offered by rich families or the systems of manorial or ceremonial lands—stressed one's place as a "community" member over class relations within the clan. Also, the cohabitation of many small families (numerous generations living together prevented any decisive rupture) gave rise to the same set of circumstances. In medieval Japan, however, familial cohesion was the product of families that had once branched and were reuniting; and the heads of the branches retained their high degree of independence as the nuclei for cohesion. This difference in how clan cohesion came about was expressed as Chinese passivity and Japanese activity.

Thus, Ishimoda argues, although there did materialize in China as well the basis for domainal or feudal production relations, the political form corresponding to these production relations did not take shape because it was restricted by clan ties. This fact applies as well to the problem of the formation of warrior bands. As witnessed by clan feuds[5] of modern times, in forging a fighting organization for village self-defense, the relationship between the commanders and the commanded could not transcend relations within the "community" of clan patriarchs and their offspring, and transform itself into personal hierarchic relations.

China developed neither domainal nor warrior relations not because she lacked the appropriate conditions; rather, those conditions existed but were restricted by the bonds in the "community" order. In Japan, feudal relations broke through such restrictions, matured rapidly, and eventually followed a distinctive historical course separate from the East Asian world. The foundation stone of modern Japan was laid here.

This comparative historical analysis of Ishimoda's raises several problems. He failed to take into account the independent role exercised by the superstructure on the base; and he tried hard to understand in a unified fashion the fulfillment of world-historical laws within the history of these two peoples as well as both peoples' unique expressions of this process.

Ishimoda developed his views more fully in his later work. In his essay, "Chūsei shi kenkyū no kiten: hōkensei e no futatsu no michi ni tsuite" (The starting point for research into medieval history: On the two paths to feudalism),[6] he argued that the T'ang was an empire of the ancient world comparable to the Roman empire, and the peoples living along China's frontiers were subsumed within this world empire. With the collapse of the T'ang empire came the individual formation of each of these nations and cultures. In this process, Japan developed from an ancient state within the orbit of the T'ang toward a feudal state. Chinese society, however, gradually underwent a serious transformation through the transition from T'ang to Five Dynasties to Sung. One aspect of the shift from ancient empire to feudal state can be seen in the decentralization of power under the system of regional commanderies and the sharply militaristic nature of it. However, the Sung dynasty, which emerged after this transitional period, took shape as a far more despotic, bureaucratic, and centralized state than any preceding dynasty. The aristocracy who had been the ruling class in ancient times collapsed precipitously, and a feudal domainal class did not crystallize as independent political forces.

Thus, the fall of the T'ang empire led to divergent paths in the development toward feudalism for the peoples of East Asia, particularly for Japan and China. Why did these two routes— the maturation of feudalism and its absence—emerge? In *Chūsei teki sekai no keisei*, Ishimoda locates the key to this in the nature of "community" relations that existed between territorial lords and peasants. Yet, the problem remains unresolved as to why China's system of territorial lords was unable to transform its ancient and "communitarian" society in the rural villages, and to construct a medieval, feudal political structure, as proved to be the case in Japan. This problem has to be addressed from an analysis of the structure of the territorial system of medieval China itself. Realizing this, Ishimoda based himself in the empirical research of Katō Shigeshi and Sudō Yoshiyuki[d] and sought to establish the nature of the Sung-Yüan period in its system of tenant farming.

In terms of their legal status, tenant farmers were free commoners, but in reality they could be bonded to a landlord. Tenant farmers were independent managers after a fashion, but they relied on the landlord for plowing oxen, farm implements, seed, fertilizer, and even housing. Thus, the tenant farmer's position was truly like that of a slave. There were no contractual tenant relations at all, but something rather closer to slavery. Ishimoda thus identified this with the early Japanese manorial system and the Colonate system of ancient Rome. In other words, it indicated a transitional phase from slavery to serfdom. Although the demise of the T'ang empire signaled a shift from slave society to serf society, China remained at a stage that could not be fully sublimated into a medieval, feudal structure.

What sort of internal linkage existed between such a system of tenant farming and the centralized, bureaucratic state structure from the Sung dynasty onward? Generally speaking, the management of landholding under the feudal system ordinarily was a bifurcation away from direct management under slavery into land tillage by peasants and land cultivation by the landlords. Under the tenant farming system, however, landlord cultivation and management of the land was fairly rare. This, at least, was Ishimoda's answer.

In Ishimoda's view, landlords under the tenant system were extraordinarily parasitic in nature. Although a widespread body of bankrupt peasants was produced by the breakup of the ancient empire, these peasants formed the pool to supply an unlimited labor power for the tenant system. Since the landlords were able to take control of the peasants through debts owed them, they were able to be parasitic in the administration of their very own land. At the same time, they were parasites in that their production relations were guaranteed by state power. In sum, without the cohesion of landlords as an independent political force vis à vis state power, the ancient state was not fully transcended but continued as a state with power centralized. Commercial and urban relations did develop and exhibited early modern[7] signs. The feudal state in China manifested a complex visage in which ancient, medieval, and early modern elements overlapped and intertwined.

This is an overall summary of Ishimoda's essay, "Chūsei shi kenkyū no kiten," which developed ideas from his book, *Chūsei teki sekai no keisei*. Particularly worthy of our attention here is that the question of the periodization from antiquity to medieval times in Chinese history was discussed through the concrete historical process of the T'ang-Sung transformation. In this connection, he attempted to prove the existence of serfdom in China on the basis of substantive production relations in a system of tenant farming. The shame associated with lack of a thoroughgoing feudal system in China, as compared with its conspicuous development in Japan, is consistent with Ishimoda's earlier work. His argument that China had followed a distinctive path to feudalism was here substantiated. As Ishimoda put it, contrary to his earlier work, which inclined toward a theory of stagnation by emphasizing the deep-rootedness of "community" relations in China, his later work aimed at breaking away from it.[8]

This desire in 1949 to disavow a theory of stagnation was

undeniably bound up with Ishimoda's corresponding position in the contemporary political scene. In the essay, "Chūsei shi kenkyū no kiten," he wrote: "The establishment of an inseparable linkage and solidarity between the advancement of the Chinese revolution and the Japanese revolution in the postwar period means that we have reached the final stage of the historical exchange between [our] two nations over a long period of time." He went on to say: "In order to understand the world-historical importance of this, we must reevaluate the historical connection between China and Japan within the history of East Asian peoples from the changing perspective of the present."

To accomplish this, Ishimoda proposed as central subjects for research: (1) the contemporary consolidation of the Chinese revolution with the Japanese revolution; (2) the mid-nineteenth century, the period in Japan of the Meiji Restoration and in China from the Taiping Rebellion through semicolonization; and, together with these two eras, (3) the period of the collapse of the empire of the ancient world in which both Japan and China established medieval feudal societies. Thus, it was Ishimoda's intention in this later work to try and capture the commonality and linkage between Chinese and Japanese history from the position of the political solidarity of the two peoples and not simply by addressing the differences in their respective societies as he had done in *Chūsei teki sekai no keisei*. This aim was, needless to say, mediated by various actual issues of the day, such as the loss of the war, the rapid successes of the Chinese revolution, and the issues of a revolution in Japan. The theoretical problem of overcoming the theory of stagnation was fixed precisely at the base point of the junction between politics and scholarship.[9]

The Development of Conceptions of Chinese Feudalism

The issues raised by Ishimoda exerted a forceful influence among historians of East Asia. He apparently fueled the tendency to pursue the development of theory by using the empirical research of other scholars. In addition to Katō Shigeshi and Sudō Yoshiyuki, there was Maeda Naonori's essay, "Higashi

Ajia ni okeru kodai no shūmatsu" (The end of the ancient period in East Asia),[10] which argued for the first time the notion that Sui and T'ang were part of antiquity.

Ishimoda's thesis was incorporated as early as 1949 into Matsumoto Shinhachirō's paper, "Genshi kodai shakai ni okeru kihon teki mujun ni tsuite" (On the fundamental contradictions in primitive and ancient societies),[11] presented at the annual meeting of the Rekishigaku kenkyūkai (The Historical Research Association). Yet, it was Nishijima Sadao's paper, "Kodai kokka no kenryoku kōzō" (The power structure of the ancient state)[12] and Hori Toshikazu's paper, "Chūgoku ni okeru hōken kokka no keitai" (The formation of the feudal state in China),[13] both delivered the following year, 1950, at the second annual meeting of the Rekishigaku kenkyūkai, which developed these issues in a scholarly, empirical manner.

Hori's paper was part of a symposium entitled "Hōken kokka no honshitsu to sono rekishi teki shokeitai"[e] (The nature of the feudal state and its historical forms); and Ishimoda offered the panel's summary report, entitled "Hōken kokka ni kansuru riron teki shomondai"[f] (Theoretical issues concerning the feudal state), which was based on the papers given by Hori and Nagahara Keiji.[14] Insofar as Chinese history was discussed, this conference is worthy of our attention, for the Rekishigaku kenkyūkai worked out its lines for research most explicitly.

One issue that came up in Ishimoda's paper was whether the centralized bureaucratic state can be regarded as a feudal state, if we consider the era from the Sung onward as medieval, for the feudal state usually assumes a decentralized state form. In his earlier essay, "Chūsei shi kenkyū no kiten," Ishimoda saw this as a relic from the ancient state, but in his 1950 paper he changed his perspective in the following way. The form of the decentralized state, he argued, is not a necessary condition of the feudal state. Even under feudalism, which assumes an anarchic political form, because the state is the mechanism for class rule, it spawns a unified segment of power. Royal power in the feudal states of Western Europe followed this pattern. Thus, it was not strange that feudal society in China constructed a centralized bureaucratic state.

The fact that this state structure was carried on after the

Sung has to be seen rather as a reflection of the severe class relations of that time. For example, there were many peasant rebellions in the transitional era from T'ang to Sung, with a high point being reached by the Huang Ch'ao[g] uprising. That uprising was on a massive scale, to which the rebellions of late antiquity in Japan could not compare, and revealed a popular energy in medieval China which had been accumulating over a long period. In the fear that these peasant uprisings could not be suppressed by the might of individual large landowners or local powers, the establishment of a centralized, bureaucratic state became a necessity.

These are the general contours of Ishimoda's paper. In sum, we should note that by stipulating that China had an "incomplete feudal state," Ishimoda set up a "Chinese form of the feudal state" in tandem with those of Western Europe and Japan. Although this theory of the Chinese feudal state was based on the contents of Hori's paper,[15] Hori's work went well together with Nishijima's paper on the ancient Chinese state. The issue Nishijima raised was the Chinese form of ancient slavery, which I would like to consider now.

Nishijima began with the following premise: when we consider the phenomenon of the ancient state, we have to assume the ruling relations of an appropriate slave system. But, since a wide variety of slave systems are predictable depending on their origins, we have to analyze both the general and the specific aspects of slave systems in history. In the past, theories of stagnation did not recognize a slave stage in China, but in order to do away with the concept of stagnation and come up with a progressive nature to Chinese society, it was necessary to recognize the existence of a period of slavery.

If there was such a Chinese form of slavery, Nishijima asked, in what way did it emerge and exist? The use of iron implements, which began in the Spring and Autumn and Warring States periods, caused an epochal development in agricultural productive power. It broke up the clan "community" that had formed the basis of the Chou "feudal" system and brought into existence a patriarchal-familial slavery. The united bodies of the clans of these patriarchal-familial slave owners were known as *hao-tsu*[h] or great clans. Family slaves were thus used to manage the land of the great clans, but with a certain limitation:

we see a "borrowed land"[16] system in the form of tenancy around the borders of the clan lands, without the evolution of a slave labor system as had been the case in classical antiquity.

On the surface, this resembles feudal serfdom and many had seen it that way in the past. However, such tenancy relations did not exist by themselves but emerged within the familial slave system. Thus, the mutually complementing structure of familial slavery and tenant farming constituted, according to Nishijima, the Chinese form of slavery.

The problem then arose as to why this particular form took shape in China. Nishijima found the answer in the nature of the imbalance in the development of productivity. The imbalance in the spread of agricultural implements made of iron gave rise to an imbalance in the development of productive power and thus did not uniformly break down the earlier clan "community." The result was that an institution from the past, the "hamlet" (*li*)[i] unit from the Han dynasty, continued to exist. Although it obstructed the diffusion of the power of the patriarchal-familial slave owners, when small peasants under this "hamlet" structure came under the rule of the great clans, these peasants were not fully enslaved but emerged as tenant farmers.

The superstructure for such a socioeconomic system was formed by the Han empire. From its very inception, however, the Han empire did not take shape as the controlling force of the great clans. In the Former Han empire, state power itself was that of a single great clan. As can be seen in the case of Liu Pang,[j] the emperor and his ministers created a structure that the great clans imitated in their relationship with their family slaves. In this sense, state power and the great clans under its control possessed the same unidimensionality, and thus the two grew into a fierce antagonism.

The Former Han, Nishijima continued, tried a variety of policies to suppress the great clans, but without success. In the Latter Han dynasty, the *hao-tsu* gained a superior hand. This is best illustrated by the changes in fiscal systems. As Katō Shigeshi had explained it, the financial structure of the Former Han was a dual system of imperial household finances and state finances; in the Latter Han, this structure was unified under the state.[17] Thus, the state shed its personalistic, great clan character and completed itself as the power mechanism of a ruling order by a collective of great clans.

The ancient Chinese state witnessed effective completion in the Latter Han dynasty, but what then is the thread that links it to the Sui-T'ang empire? Nishijima dealt with that problem as follows. Ch'in-Han society was established on the basis of an imbalance in the development of agricultural productive power; the subsequent equalization of productive power predictably removed this foundation. The "hamlet" as a vestige of the earlier clan "community" disintegrated, and the tenancy system under the control of great clans also crumbled. For the great clans this spelled a serious crisis. The great clans as a class, he went on, sensed the need for a reorganization of the structure of peasant control; and this urge was linked to the later land systems: military colonies ($t'un-t'ien$)[k] in the Three Kingdoms era, "lands in possession" ($chan-t'ien$) and "assessment lands" ($k'e-t'ien$)[18] in the Western Chin, and the equal field system of the Sui and T'ang dynasties.

Accordingly, in Nishijima's view, the Sui-T'ang period was a reorganized form of the ancient state and signified as well the final phase of the ancient state.[19] Hori's view of the feudal state also started from this conception of the Sui-T'ang empire. I should like now to consider the main points of Hori's thesis.

Hori began by reconsidering whether, as Ishimoda had argued, it was appropriate to regard the character of centralized power in the state from the Sung on merely as a reflection of a carryover from antiquity. State power from the Sung dynasty on became increasingly centralized in conjunction with the growth of a tenancy system. Thus, Hori wondered if the immaturity of this tenancy system as feudal land ownership only implied a reemergence of a system of centralized power or may have itself possessed a character demanding centralization of power.

For example, he argued, did not the extraordinarily fierce suppression of peasant rebellions, as seen in the Huang Ch'ao uprising, force the landlords to demand centralization of power? We can estimate from this the tenacity of the peasants' inclination to independence. This tenacity in the late T'ang was attributable to gradual changes within Chinese antiquity itself, for the ancient period in China took form very early on and, unlike the situation in Greece or Japan, was uninfluenced by forces from without. The T'ang was the final state in Chinese society's long ancient period. Its ruling class, the great clans, became bureaucrats and lived off the state. The "equal field" system was a structure by which the great clans depended on the state. (Hori and Nishijima agreed on the parasitic nature of the bureaucrats.)

The immensely independent nature of the peasants, which spawned the parasitic bureaucratization of the great clans, was backed by the growth in peasant productive power. Examples include the materialization of three crops biennially in North China, advances in the opening of wet-land rice paddies in Kiangnan, and the development of a general commodity circulation. These developments eventually shook up the equal field system and led to political dislocations from the mid-T'ang onward.

The emergence of regional commanderies that were military in structure with decentralized power, Hori claimed, revealed the rise of local feudal centers of power. In response to this state of affairs, the T'ang government implemented the new economic structure of the double tax and the system of monopolies. However, the regional commanderies and these new economic systems did not of themselves negate antiquity. The emergent forces that matured under this structure grew while continuing to rely on state power and ran into no basic contradictions with the T'ang dynasty.

The proletarianization of the peasantry advanced conspicuously under a dual (new and old) governance. It carried within itself severe contradictions because there was commodity circulation backing it up. The Huang Ch'ao uprising was one explosion of these contradictions, and the old aristocratic influence was exterminated. Since individual landlords were unable to restrain the energy of these peasant rebellions, the necessity emerged for a centralized state power, but the extent of the expansion of commodity circulation could not be ignored as an economic condition that enabled this to happen.

These points were the essence of Hori's paper and he reinvestigated and deepened his analysis of them in subsequent articles. He devoted particular energy to structural elucidations of peasant rebellions and the regional commanderies. In one essay, "Tōmatsu shohanran no seikaku" (The nature of rebellions in the late T'ang),[20] he argued as follows. The T'ang dynasty witnessed the bureaucratization of the aristocracy into a full grown officialdom, but this structure was shaken by the intense power struggles over bureaucratic position. These were a result of the fact that at this time the route to advancement in the world was guaranteed only by establishing a favorable relationship on an individual basis with the Son of Heaven, the despot, who stood at the pinnacle of the bureaucracy. While such court favorites came to control T'ang politics, a path toward advancement through imperial favor was opened even for non-Chinese and commoners, and this was the first step in the dismemberment of the aristocratic system. The An Lu-shan[l] Rebellion arose from a power struggle among such court favorites, as can be seen in the opposition between An Lu-shan, a man of non-Chinese origins, and Yang Kuo-chung,[m] a man of commoner background.

The link between the emperor and his favorites at court, Hori continued, was based on a personal connection. This same kind of personal bond can be found in the internal structure of An Lu-shan's power as well as that of other regional commanderies. The best illustration of this is the fictive family ties of "adopted son" or "sworn brothers" which linked the military governor to his troops. An Lu-shan, for example, had his own private army of eight thousand non-Chinese "adopted sons," and he additionally supported a "family army" of over one thousand men as attendants. Thus, the nucleus of a military governor's troops possessed a fictive familial structure in which the autocratic control of the regional commander was rendered thoroughgoing by the personal protection and favors offered the troops. In one respect, this might be seen as relations of slavery.

After the An Lu-shan Rebellion, a semi-independent regional commandery appeared north of the Yellow River, and in fighting with the T'ang dynasty it succeeded in gaining powers of territorial inheritance, control of tax collection, and the freedom to appoint and dismiss officials. At the same time, the internal structure of the regional commandery was exposed to the danger of a ceaseless overpowering of superiors by inferiors. The military governor was always left open to the danger of being toppled by the troops under his command. Thus, because the military governor's position was extremely unstable, he was unable to cut his ties with the central power. While the regional commandery structure of the T'ang spawned personal bonds of cohesion, in the end it could not overcome the ancient bureaucratic system.

The Huang Ch'ao uprising destroyed this dependency between the regional commanderies and the T'ang court. Huang Ch'ao's insurgent forces were composed of an immense number of impoverished, displaced persons and centered around heroic types who harbored a discontent for the contemporary political state of affairs. Since these bands of roaming banditti did not aim at overthrowing the T'ang dynasty and were poorly organized, even though they did succeed in capturing Ch'ang-an, they were headed straight for destruction. Although Huang Ch'ao's forces had these weaknesses, they still destroyed the T'ang and made possible the independence of regional commanderies. Thus was born the Five Dynasties period.

Hori concluded his analysis as follows. Why was it that China did not produce a feudal political structure but rather assumed the form of inferiors supplanting superiors (i.e., the bureaucracy) if the tenancy system was regarded as serfdom? Although the starting point of feudalism, the lord-vassal relationship, was a personal protective bond in the early period, it rose to the status of official authority with the security of landholding. While feudalism arose as the mutual relations of landowners and it acquired public authority as the preserver of the social order, when this feudal system matured from within ancient society, it negated and finally toppled the ancient bureaucratic order in which the ancient great clans, large local landowners, were the apex of the hierarchy.[21] Nonetheless, it was impossible for a feudal political structure to be formed in China because of its complete bureaucratic system and the aristocracy that lived totally off the bureaucracy. Without being brought to an end, the bureaucracy inclined toward a mode that would change in accord with the rising of inferiors to oust their superiors.

In short, according to Hori, a feudal political structure did not materialize in China because of the thoroughness of the bureaucratic system. Although this development was predicated on the expansion of productive power, such a growth did not necessarily accompany the historical newness of this personalized structure in the political and military spheres. Thus, it could not sweep away fictive familial slave relations, and the structure of the patriarchal-familial slave system, as Nishijima had described Ch'in-Han society, was, if not revitalized, unable to be overturned.

In Nishijima's view, the ruling structure of Ch'in-Han society centered around patriarchal-familial slavery with peasants living in "communities" outside this system. These two forms of mutually complementing ties among the people constituted for Nishijima in concrete form the ancient Chinese slave system. Hori later dealt with this issue in two detailed essays: "Kō Sō no hanran: Tōmatsu henkakki no ichi kōsatsu" (The Huang Ch'ao uprising: A study of the changing times at the end of the T'ang),[22] and "Hanchin shin'eigun no kenryoku kōzō" (The power structure of the personal defense forces in the regional commanderies).[23]

In these two essays, Hori strove to support more fully the main points of his earlier work. He analyzed power in the regional commanderies and the groups in the Huang Ch'ao rebellion, both of which emerged as the antithesis of the ancient bureaucratic system of the T'ang. And, he looked at the internal power structure of rich merchants and strong local families who may have controlled the authority of these two groups (regional commanderies and Huang Ch'ao rebel bands) and who later, from the Sung on, became the mainstays of the centralized bureaucratic state. Hori argued that patriarchal-familial slave relations made up the central element of their authority. Examples include the regional commander and his personal defense forces army, Huang Ch'ao and his immediate family and protégés, or the locally powerful families (heads of estates) and their workers. Outside this central system of relations were mercenary troops, impoverished peasants, and perhaps a class of villagers.

Relations in these peripheral groups make one think of the actual human control, in the form of two bonds, that the ancient state exerted on self-cultivating peasants. These bonds—one personal, one official—differed in form, but both were ties of slavery in the sense that there was a unilinear control of superiors over inferiors and of actual human control unmediated through land. Although the regional command-eries destroyed the official bonds of control that were the basis of the T'ang legal system by creating these personal cohesive bonds, they also relied on them. Thus, these personal bonds were insufficient to build their own political structure—a feudal political structure—by subsuming the official bonds; and in a sense they allowed the founding of a centralized bureaucratic state, itself a revival of the ancient state.

So went Hori's argument. However immature were the two strata of locally powerful families and rich merchants who controlled the state, they ran the tenancy system, which was a feudal mode of production. In this sense, he argued, the period from the Five Dynasties and Sung on should be considered a feudal era in China.[24]

Logical Contradictions in the Conceptions of Feudalism

As we have seen, the issues raised shortly after the war by Ishimoda Shō were picked up by Nishijima Sadao and Hori Toshikazu, who pursued empirically the study of slavery in China, the forms it took, and its transition to feudalism. It was their substantive intention to try and overturn the "theory of stagnation" by showing that Chinese society had developed according to the laws of world history. Were they successful?

Characteristic of Nishijima's and Hori's theses was the at-tempt to demonstrate the progressive nature of Chinese history by applying the two theoretical categories for world history—slavery and feudalism—to the concrete historical process from Ch'in-Han to T'ang-Sung times. Both men, of course, did not feel that these categories could be applied to Chinese history in their ideal forms. They argued that slavery was limited to a patriarchal-familial slave system and *did not develop* into the system of slave labor that we see in classical antiquity in the West. It was hence a limited slavery. On the issue of the forma-tion of feudalism as well, they concluded that it was limited to the patriarchal structure and the centralized bureaucratic state, *without having produced* the mutual lord-vassal bond mediated by fidelity and obligation, as we see in the medieval West, or the feudal political structure built on this bond.

This was how they dealt with the distinctiveness of slavery and feudalism in China. It is noteworthy that both men expressed themselves only in a negative fashion with respect to these issues. I would like to address this problem a little more fully now.

According to the "theory of stagnation," which both men sought to overcome, the European world and the non-European world differed in their historical dispositions. It claimed that the former was by nature progressive and the latter by nature stagnant. Thus, the yardstick of history was placed in the European world. Nishijima and Hori tried to show that the principles of progress common to the European world were fundamentally realized in Chinese society. The more they worked at demonstrating this proposition, the more the essential Chinese social realities proved lacking. In his discussion of the Ch'in-Han empire, for example, Nishijima argued that the slave system, a product of the dissolution of "communities," was a progressive element, and on this basis he set the historical stipulations of the Ch'in-Han empire. Yet, the "communitarian" universe of the wide body of small, self-cultivating peasantry who supported the empire itself could only impede the development toward the prototypical slave system and thus presented an obstruction. In other words, the era could only be cast in the role of a shadow to the light. Hence, it was merely a vestige of an earlier era lagging behind, which prevented the full development of its progressive essence.

The same can roughly be said about Hori's work. While he focused on a variety of the elements of a new era—regional commanderies, the tenancy system, rebel groups, and so on— which arose in the late T'ang, from the perspective of European feudalism China could only be assigned the role of an expression of the underdevelopment of feudalism. The realities of history seemed to be missing. For example, unable to locate just what it was that Huang Ch'ao was trying to conquer, Hori ended up offering a structural analysis mainly from the point of view discussed earlier.

Furthermore, the problem of the formation of the centralized state was only assigned significance by Hori as the mechanism of repression against an intensely independent peasantry, whereas the actual content of the world formed by the peasantry—this may have provided the structural foundations for the centralized state—was scarcely considered. His calling the centralized state a feudal state was based on the recognition that the tenancy system, which was characterized as serfdom, formed its cornerstone. Its import as a feudal state originated merely in the abstract sense that it was the preservative mechanism for serfdom.

Why was it that the European feudal state of the Middle Ages took a decentralized form? As Hori said, this was owing to the form in which the ancient empire was transcended. If this is so, then to the extent that the centralized bureaucratic state in China from the Sung is considered a form of the feudal state, should he not have to demonstrate in the same way that this was the form of transcendence over China's antiquity? But, Hori continued to argue that China had not been able to overcome the ancient empire fully. Thus, his designation of it as a feudal state was not the result of an analysis of the state itself (the superstructure), but its economic base, the tenancy system, which he understood as serfdom. Although his efforts to apply the principles of historical materialism to Chinese history were acknowledged, he actually made a comprehensive understanding of Chinese history more difficult.

Roughly speaking, the efforts of both Nishijima and Hori to overcome theories of stagnation were unable in the final analysis to go beyond the framework of Western European historical formulations. When both men sought to fix the entirety of Chinese society upon the basis of the common elements of Chinese and Western societies, the elements most basic to Chinese society had to fall through their sieve. This basic difference between Chinese society and that of the West lay in the enduring existence of "communal" society among the small, self-cultivating peasantry. This obstructed, even perverted, the overall structural development on which was predicated private systems of ownership, slavery, and serfdom.

Not that either of them failed to recognize this problem, for Nishijima had included "community" ties as one part of the social structure of slavery. But, when they attempted to explain the progressive nature of Chinese society with slavery and serfdom as historical prescriptions, the world of the "community" finally had to be driven into a negative position and theoretically abstracted. It was the obstinate persistence of this world of the "community" upon which had been based a notion of stagnancy in Chinese society. In the final analysis, Nishijima and Hori had been unsuccessful in their objective of transcending the conception of stagnation, itself the height of Europocentrism. And here we see one of the barriers with which postwar historiography collided.

Of course, Nishijima and Hori are not the only ones to be blamed in this regard. Conceptions of slavery and feudalism faced an inevitable dilemma any time one tried to grasp Chinese history in its totality. One such theory was put forward by the late Niida Noboru, who shortly after the war argued that China was a feudal society from the Sung dynasty onward. He presented his thesis in its most complete form in his essay, "Chūgoku shakai no 'hōken' to fyūdarizumu" (*Feng-chien* and feudalism in Chinese society).[25] I shall now discuss Niida's theory of feudalism, making reference primarily to this essay but also to other articles included in his major work, *Chūgoku hōsei shi kenkyū* (Studies in Chinese legal history).

Niida began his essay with this statement: "Feudal (medieval) society, i.e., serf society, comprises one social formation in the stages of development, i.e., a historical category." The prescription that saw medieval, feudal, and serf society as synonymous and as one of the universal stages of development shows that Niida shared Ishimoda's and Hori's conception of feudalism and their theoretical underpinnings. From this position, Niida argued as follows. Three points were of major importance in formulating the feudal stage in Chinese history in the manner cited: (1) it constituted a critique of the notion of stagnancy in Chinese society; (2) it made possible an overall structure for a world history, East and West; and (3) it offered a scientific explanation for the modern Chinese revolution as an antifeudal struggle. Niida's ways of attaching significance to these ideas of Chinese feudalism indicate the currents of thought he shared with others at the time rather than his own unique conceptions.

In any case, Niida sought to establish the period for feudalism in Chinese history. The prime feature of Chinese feudalism, as might be predicted from his definition, was considered to be tenant farming as a system of serfdom. Thus, the T'ang-Sung transition, from the eighth to the tenth centuries, marked the dividing line between antiquity and medieval times. Prior to the T'ang, slaves and not fully enslaved tenant farmers (these designations are based on Nishijima's conceptions) were the basic agricultural labor force under the management of large land-holders known as *yu-hsing ta-tsu*[n] (great clans). Niida recognized the quantitative prevalence of slavery as well, but he argued that the rise in productive capacity in the T'ang caused slave production to develop into serf production, and it brought about the emergence of a new stratum of large landlord-bureaucrats who replaced the *yu-hsing ta-tsu* who had stood over the slave system.

The most typical expression of this serfdom was what Niida called *zuiden denkyaku*[o] (land-bound tenancy). When a landlord disposed of land, tenant farmers of this sort were turned over to the buyer along with the land. Thus, they were bound to the land of large landlords and lacked the freedom to change their place of residence. They differed from slaves, however, in that whereas a slave submitted to the unspecified and unlimited control of his owner and was obliged to labor without compensation, the tenant farmer submitted to the somewhat more specified control of a master, owned his own means of production, lived according to his own calculations, and thus a part of his labor was his own. Landlord control over tenants was an indirect control in which land served as an intermediary, not a form of direct control over their very person, as in a slave system.

Niida's and others' analyses of tenancy relied to a considerable extent on the research of Sudō Yoshiyuki,[26] but Niida worked particularly hard at reinforcing the tenancy-serfdom thesis from the angle of legal history. According to Sung law, he argued, the status of a tenant farmer was carefully worked out: between a landlord and tenant there existed a "master-servant" relationship; and the law governing the general populace did not apply to adultery between a landlord and the womenfolk of a tenant. Thus, although the tenant farmer differed from the slave or the *pu-ch'ü* or the higher ranks of the poor, he still did not have the same legal status as the general populace.

The tenancy system itself, however, underwent historical development. Niida argued that changes were apparent in tenancy between two eras: the early medieval Sung-Yüan period and the later medieval Ming-Ch'ing period. For example, Ming and Ch'ing law did not make provision for inequality between tenant and owner, so that the punishment for tenant violence against a landlord was no different from that of the general populace. Nor in cases of adultery between landlords and the women of a tenant household was the status of the tenant afforded particular attention, as it had been in the Sung; it was treated in the same way as cases involving the population at large. Furthermore, whereas in the Sung they stressed a "master-servant" relationship between landlord and tenant, in the Ming and Ch'ing the ritual of the "younger serving the older" (*i shao shih chang*)[p] became the model for this relationship. The latter case meant that they had merely fixed a metaphorical relationship on the basis of age, while the status relationship disappeared.

According to Niida, this development—from a status tenancy system to a nonstatus tenancy system—revealed a stage in which the bonds of the tenant-serf were being overcome. (He argued they were finally destroyed by the modern Chinese revolution.) Yet he pointed out that behind this development was a multiplicity of peasant rebellions, bond servant uprisings (so-called *nu-pien*),[q] and rent-resistance movements in the Ming and Ch'ing. Thus, the struggle of tenant farmers against the landlords' undue influence by law and the increase in tenant might caused the tenancy system to change into a nonstatus relationship, and this struggle ran through the modern Chinese revolution from the Taiping rebellion onward.

What were the distinguishing characteristics Niida assigned to Chinese feudalism? As we have noted, he cited a "master-servant" relationship between landlord and tenant, and claimed that Sung Neo-Confucianism systematized the idea of this "relationship" as a general ethic in human relations. Like pre-Sung Confucian thought, Sung Neo-Confucianism regarded as absolute the control of sovereign over subject and father over son, and it considered the Five Human Relationships centering on these two to be everlasting, immutable truth. One of the further characteristics of Sung Neo-Confucianism was the effort to ground this immutable truth in the "heavenly principle" (*t'ien-li*)[r] or natural law of a universal order. To understand all human relations as established a priori by this heavenly principle was in fact the idea of being contented with one's place in the world (*shou-fen*).[s] By rigidifying the sovereign/father–subject/son relationship, Sung Neo-Confucianism aimed at stabilizing the existing social order.

In this manner, Niida understood Sung Neo-Confucianism to be the intellectual formulation of a feudal ideology, but he also noted that it had the following traits. Sung Neo-Confucianism advocated the obligation of the subject or son to repay the kindness bestowed on him by the sovereign or father. The emphasis placed on the bond between this kindness and its repayment did not indicate that the control exercised by a sovereign or father over his subject or son was necessarily unconditional, but that to a certain extent a mutual relationship existed. However, the consciousness in which this kindness of sovereign or father was called for and the consciousness of power that seemed to overlay this kindness were conspicuous. They were not terribly far from effectively expressing a conception of unconditional control.

Niida argued that this was owing to the patriarchal authority that had been inherited from antiquity, and these were not feudal bonds of the medieval European kind. One of the characteristics of medieval European feudalism was that the sovereign-subject bond was a contractual and legal relationship entered into by independent parties with conditions placed on both sides, whereas medieval China lacked the freedom of consciousness in this sense. The controlling bond of the blood-line patriarch made a two-sided relationship one-sided.

In this connection, Niida severely criticized the view that equated the Chou *feng-chien* system with medieval European feudalism. Although the two systems were similar in that sovereign and subject were linked by a relationship in which the former "enfeoffed" the latter, this was merely a superficial similarity. What supported *feng-chien* ties in the Chou period were natural ties of blood. In China, this patriarchal bond functioned as a controlling tie and later regulated the societies of ancient and medieval times. Accordingly, Chinese society in this sense may not have experienced feudalism. But, Niida went on to argue: "This control itself [patriarchal control] does not mean that medieval Chinese society lacked a feudal base—serfdom. I shall test for the existence of feudalism in medieval China on the grounds of whether such a base existed." [27] In other words, the existence itself of serfdom, he claimed, was the key to resolving unmistakably whether feudalism had existed or not.

We have now discussed in general terms Niida Noboru's ideas on feudalism. But no explanation was forthcoming when it came to describing the nature of the link tying the patriarchal structure as a system of control with the tenancy system as the feudal base. Generally speaking, we are left with the impression that this problem had been discarded without any attempt to unify the general progressive aspects of Chinese society with its particular stagnating elements. This is most clearly indicated by the following statement of Niida's. Having noted the lack in China of a contractual bond between sovereign and subject as, Niida claimed, had existed in European feudalism, he added this conclusion: "From these points, *we can only deny that feudalism existed in Chinese society*. However, there is no need to force feudalism narrowly into the mold of European feudal society. European and Japanese feudalism are only one type of feudalism. Might we not say in a broad sense that the Chinese case illustrates yet another type?" [28]

This was clearly a rather careless statement. The points of Niida's argument cited earlier indicate that we were aware his theory of feudalism shared the same dilemma as Hori's. That is, by fixing a period of feudalism in China, he was promoting the notion that Chinese society was part of a world historical universality, but he was then faced with the underdevelopment of feudalism in China. In order to deal with this problem, Niida stressed the existence of a serf system in feudalism at the societal base (the tenancy system), but this made it difficult to explain how such a base conformed to the superstructure (the bonds of control) from the Sung dynasty onward.

Ishimoda (in his book, *Chūsei teki sekai no keisei*) and Nishijima had considered the remnants of strongly rooted "community" ties as something that inhibited the typical development of slavery and feudalism in China. How did Niida deal with this issue? In his essay, "Chūgoku no dōzoku mata wa sonraku no tochi shoyū mondai" (Chinese clans and the problem of village land ownership),[29] Niida claimed that the tenth and eleventh centuries were a great turning point in the history of "communities" too. In this period, various groups with a new historical consciousness emerged and grew to replace the ancient kinship groups and gave medieval society its distinctive character. Guilds were one of these new groups, as were reconstructed clan groupings. The latter were characterized by their mutual aid activities through a system of clan lands (charitable estates, ceremonial lands, etc.).

These clans can be seen particularly in central and South China, and in the final analysis they were the mainstay of the large landlord system of the day. He argued that the landlord, fearful lest class differentiation within the clan disrupt the feudal ruling system, provided these mutual aid functions in order to stabilize the feudal order by stabilizing the villagers' livelihood. Furthermore, there was also the aim of returning profits to the clan by offering educational funds from the charitable estate revenues to promising sons, which enabled them to sit for the examinations and allowed as many as possible among them to become officials. In this way, the system of clan lands was inseparably bound together with landlord control. The significance of the reorganization of clan groupings, Niida concluded, lay in stabilizing the social order through the landlord system.

We know from the plethora of clan genealogies[30] that clan groups existed in various places from the Sung dynasty on, and that they set clan regulations and operated mutual aid functions, as Niida pointed out. He used these materials to discuss in detail the structure and function of clan groupings. He showed that, in addition to the communal management of charitable estates and ceremonial lands, clans exclusively ran such operations as the fertilization of fields with cut grass, irrigation, and cemeteries through control over ties of acceptance into the clan. When a conflict of interest arose with another clan, they did not hesitate to use force (as in clan feuds). On the use of the power over acceptance into membership in the clan, "communitarian" regulations were in effect internally so that, for example, the allocation of time and the quantity to be harvested were set in the grass fertilization that were communal land. Stipulations were even added for produce from private hills and forests (such as rules for the harvest time of bamboo shoots, tea leaves, and camellia blossoms).

The clan "community" was the arena for the regeneration of the livelihoods of individual clan members, and its management was undertaken by a system involving the head of the clan. Clan heads were known by such names as *tsung-tzu*,[t] *tsu-chang*,[u] *tsung-chang*,[v] and *tsu-cheng*,[w] sometimes alternately, but in any case their power transcended that of any individual family or its head, the patriarch, as they assumed control over the entire clan body. Their duties included clan ceremonies, resolution of disputes within the clan, and sanctions against those who violated clan regulations. Clan members were obliged to follow the orders of the clan head, but the clan head also had to follow the clan regulations and be upright and honest with the clan. In cases where the clan head himself acted improperly, he might be recalled by members of the clan. Cases where this power of recall were clearly recorded in the clan rules are not rare. Thus, the clan head did not possess the qualification of merely being a clan elder; he had to be sufficiently moral to earn the popularity of the clan members.

This should indicate that clan cohesion was based not merely on vertical ties of control and submission, but that horizontal ties of companionship and solidarity were also at work. One issue in this connection is the situation of the individual families within a clan. Although clan ties tended to supersede the independence of individual families, this is not unrelated to the lack, which Niida noted, of dominance, exclusiveness, and absoluteness of the patriarch's power. The principle of the equal distribution of family property also caused the weakening of the patriarch's power. Thus, the Chinese family itself was not permeated by vertical ties of control and submission, but showed a diffusion of power and privilege among the individual members of the family. (According to Niida, allocations of family property were strictly observed for women as well. In the Kiangsu-Anhwei region in the Southern Sung, women inherited one-half as much as men.) Such circumstances seem to indicate the fact that the lack of complete family cohesion enabled individual family units to form ties of clan cohesion, that is, horizontal bonds of solidarity.

As we have now seen, Niida argued that the historical significance of clan cohesion was the policy of stabilizing the social
order on the basis of the large landlord system. Yet, as Niida
himself described in detail, the clan was well furnished with a
"communitarian" nature and was understood as embodying an
autonomous system of regulation in village life among the
people. Although we speak of large landholders, elders, and
clan heads within clans, we cannot ignore this system of regulation. Seeing it only as a means of stabilizing the social order
under large landlords will inevitably lead to a superficial view.
In spite of this, Niida remained stubbornly committed to this
position derived from his argument that the social bonds of the
day were based on his tenancy-serfdom thesis. After he described the "communitarian" reality of clan cohesion, Niida
concluded: "In any case, however, clan cohesion was the mainstay of the large landlord system. It served the function of
stabilizing the feudal order and the village order through clan
self-interest and was a means for the large landlords to use the
peasantry." [31] He scarcely looked at the internal structure that
linked "communitarian" bonds and bonds of the landlord
system. One cannot escape the feeling that he forced a linkage
between the two only at the level of words.

Disputation Over Conceptions of Feudalism

As we have thus far seen, the primary basis from which
Ishimoda, Hori, and Niida around 1950 derived their conceptions of Chinese feudalism was tenancy as a system of feudal serfdom. Although they pursued the tenancy-serfdom-
feudalism proposition, they still left something unaccounted for
in Chinese society of the post-Sung era. They encountered the
same problem as the inability to explain the Ch'in-Han empire
with the category of slavery, for the greatest difficulty lay in
comprehending China's distinctive superstructure, despotic
state power. The state from the Sung dynasty forward was a
system of "monarchical autocracy"—a bureaucratic state in
which power was highly concentrated. Hori's arguments were
not persuasive as to how the tenancy system, as serfdom, corresponded to this. If tenancy did not beget a "feudal political
structure," then we must investigate whether tenancy actually

constituted the reality of serfdom. This leads to questions about the bases themselves on which these conceptions of feudalism were formed. Thus, clearly an explanation of serfdom in conjunction with the centralized state subsumes this major dilemma surrounding conceptions of feudalism.

Niida dealt with this issue by claiming that we see the existence and even the decentralization of bodies with a closed nature, such as guilds and clan villages, from Sung times on. However, he did not address at all whether this tendency toward decentralization gave state power itself a decentralized feudal character. As we have noted, in order to formulate a notion of feudalism, not only the socioeconomic base but also the overall social structure that this base created through mutual interaction with the superstructure must be demonstrated as having nothing short of a feudal organization. The conceptions of feudalism that emerged around 1950, though, were problematic in this regard and in actuality ushered a host of problems into the scholarly world.

First, on the question of tenancy, Miyazaki Ichisada offered an opposing thesis[32] to Sudō Yoshiyuki's explanation that had been considered a convincing basis for a theory of feudalism. Leader of the so-called Kyoto school of sinology, Miyazaki understood the T'ang-Sung transition as the movement from medieval to modern times; this response to Sudō was one part of the view in which he saw tenancy in this period as a modern tenant system. Miyazaki's main points included the following: (1) Although the medieval estates through the T'ang formed large unified entities in China, from the Sung on shrinkage in the size of plots increased owing to the breakup of ownership rights. (2) As a result, the landlord's bond to the tenant ceased to be of a territorial, personal nature, and the two became linked by economic, contractual ties. (3) Existing documents that seem to provide evidence that tenants were forcibly bound to the land may have been a means merely to prevent tenants from discarding contracts and leaving the land, or perhaps to ensure for landlords whose local work force was insufficient that they would have manpower. (4) The existence in the Southern Sung of two-layered tenancy rights (landlord-usufructuary-cultivator) indicates the establishment of usufructuary rights on the land. Sudō wrote a response, but we shall put aside for a moment the issue of whether his understanding of tenancy was correct, for the major advantages of Miyazaki's thesis were that he was able to explain how the base and the superstructure conformed to each other.

The well-known periodization of the Kyoto school, put forth by Naitō Konan,ˣ designated the era through the Han as ancient (*jōko*),ʸ through the T'ang as medieval (*chūko*),ᶻ and from the Sung on as modern. One of the differences between medieval and modern times, he argued, was between aristocratic government and monarchical-autocratic government. In the former, an aristocratic class ruled the people by virtue of its personal and status qualities, and the sovereign was merely the common property of this aristocratic class.

The T'ang-Sung transformation, however, swept away aristocratic rule. The newly formed monarchical autocracy linked the ties of power between the sovereign and the people directly, without the intermediary of the aristocracy. This change also spelled the extinction of rule by status or personal quality. Thus, in the periodization of Chinese history offered by the Kyoto school of sinology, the T'ang-Sung transition removed medieval bonds and gave rise to a new stage of history. Miyazaki saw the tenancy system as one of small cultivators who emerged at this new point in history—modern society. This system was understood as a contractual, nonstatus economic structure that corresponded to the superstructure of monarchical autocracy.

Miyazaki's position was a critique aimed directly at the thesis that this tenancy system constituted serfdom, and Sudō took up the gauntlet. Later, various views were raised surrounding this debate, and critiques by both sides were exchanged, but the final results remain unclear.[33] However, this situation shows at least that the idea that the tenancy system was serfdom has ceased to be generally accepted among scholars. Even those who had argued the case for feudalism now began entertaining misgivings about equating Chinese tenancy with the Western conception of serfdom.[34]

In another approach, Chinese society from the Sung dynasty on was examined in an area somewhat different from the nature of tenancy. Attention was focused on the problem of whether we can unmistakably deduce the overall nature of society simply from the tenancy system of private management. Concretely speaking, attention focused on the social arena that superseded individual management or generalized it—village society. One study in this vein was Yanagida Setsuko's "Kyōsonsei no tenkai" (The development of the village system).[35] While agreeing with the notion that the landlord-tenant system embodied the basic production relations from the Sung forward, Yanagida argued that state power at this time did not materialize simply and directly on top of these relations of production without any intermediary. Her point was that local villages, as the bases of control by state power, were not completely covered by this landlord-tenant bond alone. The system of large landholdings that took form at the end of the T'ang could not absorb all the impoverished peasants from the equal field system as tenants and could not mold manor society on a nationwide basis. Thus, a majority of middle-level and small landowners (double tax households)[36] who could not be incorporated into the large landholding system existed widely throughout Chinese villages. These self-cultivating peasants needed horizontal, mutually cohesive bonds in order to support themselves. In other words, Yanagida argued that there existed simultaneously a vertical control relationship between landlord and tenant as well as this horizontal bond of solidarity; it remained necessary, in her view, to elucidate how these two relations intertwined to form the basis for state power.

Yanagida's proposition did not necessarily, of itself, conflict with a conception of feudalism. But, if we compare it to Niida's view of the clan village (discussed earlier), the originality of her position becomes clearer. In Niida's view, clan cohesion (i.e., "community") was only a means of control over the tenancy system. According to Yanagida, however, village cohesion (i.e., "community") was a different sort of social bond than that of tenancy, and she pointed to how this cohesion in the village interlocked—namely, the formation of its internal bonds—as a problem that need be addressed. Thus, the thesis that China from the Sung dynasty on was feudal was still incomplete for Yanagida. With future research on the problems she raised, we can fully anticipate an unknown world to unfold.

When we predict the existence of an unknown world in Chinese history, what is first of all assumed is the world of the "community," which appears in many and varied forms. It is the strongest opponent of theories of Chinese feudalism (as well as theories of Chinese slavery), as I have mentioned several times. Both Nishijima and Hori later came to understand this.

As is well known, Nishijima withdrew his ideas from around 1950, after receiving a number of critiques, and thereafter built a thesis of the Ch'in-Han empire around new conceptions. His new position did not see the Ch'in-Han empire as a ruling structure based on slavery, but hypothesized the empire as an extended form of the "communitarian" order made up of self-managing peasants. Hori seems recently to have become deeply concerned with looking for the foundations of state power of the Sui and T'ang in "communitarian" bonds as one side of the great clan system. One example is his view that the equal field system restrained the large landholdings of the great clans by the state's assuming control over the "communitarian" order of the peasant village that had been under great clan control.[37] In the next section, I would like to look at whether such a perspective is appropriate, but for now it seems as though this "community" is not simply the residue of the past but the foundation for the formation of the state.

This change in Nishijima's and Hori's views influenced conceptions of feudalism in a major way. In particular, the debate over Nishijima's earlier thesis and his subsequent repudiation of it gave rise to profound doubts about how well understood the "slave period" was in Chinese history. This in turn struck a severe blow at the new postwar intellectual system by raising the problem of a method with which to understand Chinese history. It spelled the end of "the postwar period"[38] for Chinese historical research. In the next chapter, we shall look at the situation that followed the one just described.

Three

The Evolution of Critiques of Theories of Unilinear Development and the Problem of Feudalism

"Modernization" Theory and the Problem of Reevaluating Feudalism

By the middle of the 1950s, it became evident that the effort to understand Chinese history in world historical terms with general categories such as slavery and serfdom had run into severe theoretical as well as empirical difficulties. This situation spawned a movement that emphasized the particularity of Chinese history. In substantive terms, this constituted a trend toward stressing the despotic nature of Chinese society and trying to find the basic class relations between the autocratic state and the masses. The perspective that saw class differentiation among the people as giving rise to fundamental class relations and thus defining the historical nature of that society began to retreat into the background. Although the new trend did not completely deny the phenomenon of class differentiation among the people, it was given a secondary, subordinate position.

Nishijima's new position was already an expression of this trend, and we should note here that this trend was rather strongly reflected in the understanding of the history of the Six Dynasties period. The historical character of Six Dynasties society was considered to be the old aristocratic system. It was thought, for example, that the Six Dynasties aristocrats existed in a transcendent position over state power, or rather that state power was a collegial organ of the aristocratic class, a perpetual ruling class that led society. Thus each dynasty in this era was merely a temporary power. This view of the aristocracy in Six Dynasties society appeared before the war. Needless to say, it was the position of the Kyoto school founded by Naitō Konan. Also, because it was based on the historical research of the Ch'ing school of textual criticism, it expressed in this sense a traditional Chinese historiographical orthodoxy.

The Kyoto school's thesis that the Six Dynasties constituted China's medieval period is based in this conception of the aristocratic system. Nishijima's earlier position understood the Six Dynasties aristocracy as a bureaucratic aristocratization of the ancient great clans, namely patriarchal slave owners. Although this conception is distant from the Kyoto school's thesis of a medieval aristocracy, they do share in the view that the Six Dynasties aristocracy was an independent class that possessed (or had once possessed) the source of power some-where within society. Yano Chikara's[aa] and Ochi Shigeaki's[ab] theses on the Six Dynasties, which appeared around the time that Nishijima retreated from his earlier position, heralded a new trend in that they did not firmly recognize the independence of the Six Dynasties aristocracy as a class. Let us take a look at the general contours of their ideas.

Yano analyzed the economic livelihood of influential aristo-crats in the Wei-Chin period. He felt that many of them had been stipendiaries of the state and that the Six Dynasties aristo-crats were bureaucrats who lived off the state just as had officials in the Ch'in-Han period. They were what Max Weber called patrimonial bureaucrats, merely dependents of the sovereign. Within such a structure, this fact was the sole arena of power; and just as in the Han empire, the state was basic to the houses of the Six Dynasties. Even in the Southern Dy-nasties, where the aristocratic system was held in reverence, the emperor's position, Yano argued, was secure as a political absolute with respect both to individual aristocrats and the aristocratic system.

Ochi Shigeaki's view of the Six Dynasties was different in nuance from Yano's, but they were in agreement in emphasiz-ing the parasitic-bureaucratic side of the Six Dynasties aristocracy. Ochi argued that at the same time that they possessed this bureaucratic side, the Six Dynasties literati played an independent role as socially renowned families through the Wei and Western Chin eras; from the Eastern Chin on, however, the bureaucratic side expanded until they became parasitic officials fully dependent on state power. Corresponding to this, imperial power eliminated the special privileges of the aristocratic class and moved toward a thorough, unitary, personal control.

What was the importance of Yano's and Ochi's arguments? In a word, they expressed doubts about using the aristocratic system as the historical index to the Six Dynasties era. If they could prove their point, then the entirety of Chinese history might be described with the schema of despotic power controlling the masses. If their positions are so presented, the implication is that they have assumed a negative attitude toward understanding Chinese history as developmental stages in a historical structure, such as ancient-slave or medieval-feudal society.

I have analyzed this issue elsewhere,[39] and I shall not offer an assessment here. The reason I particularly raise this notion of theirs is that it seems as though it fully tended toward the view of world history that emerged in the latter half of the 1950s. This tendency was critical of the unilinear development theories, which were the hallmark of the postwar understanding of world history, and it arose vigorously outside, rather than from within, the scholarly world of East Asian studies. Furthermore, it was not generated and circulated in Japan alone but constituted a new intellectual trend with impact on an international scale. Not merely an academic problem concerning our comprehension of Chinese history, as might be expected, it contained very serious contemporary problems directly linked to world politics. Although I do not preclude the possibility of overstepping the bounds of the issues in this section, I should like to try and give a general overview of this new trend.

One example representative of this trend was Umesao Tadao's "Bunmei no seitai shikan josetsu" (Introduction to a historical view of the forms of civilization).[40] Another would be Edwin O. Reischauer's collection of essays entitled *Nihon kindai no atarashii mikata* (A new approach to modern Japan).[41] Both these works dealt with questions that consumed the journalistic world in Japan from the late 1950s through the early 1960s. Since I have already discussed elsewhere[42] the problem of how these two men understand feudalism, I shall avoid too deeply trespassing at this point on old turf. But, from the perspective of the postwar trend to conceptualize world history, both of these men's ideas were direct challenges to the unilinear development theories that had held a dominant position until then in the Japanese academic world.

For example, Ueyama Shumpei[ac] had earlier expressed dissatisfaction with the conception of unilinear development current among Marxists (the view that the developmental process of human society was a one-lane road from primitive communism, to slavery, to feudalism, through capitalism, and then to socialism); and he sought the possibility for harmony between the Marxist world view and a multiform view of history.[43] When Umesao proposed his thesis advocating a multiform conception of history, he praised Ueyama's idea and called for Marxists to accept it.

Beside the historical course within civilization—Umesao's "first zone"—which followed exactly the stages from antiquity to medieval times (feudalism) to modernity (capitalism), Umesao posited the existence within civilization of a "second zone," in which this spontaneous succession did not transpire. The latter was the zone in which ancient civilization originally flourished; and, the rise of the ancient state in the first zone was due to the spread of ancient civilization into the second zone— merely its imitation. However, although the second zone caused the emergence of feudalism in the first zone and was linked to the generation of modernity later, it showed no conspicuous historical development because huge despotic empires continued to rise and fall. Thus, without a distinctive historical stage of feudalism being clearly demarcated, the second zone stumbled and fell along the wayside in the modernization process of world history. This modernization effort showed a marked trend toward the building of a sense of group along communistic or socialistic lines, not to be accomplished by the bourgeoisie, as in the first zone, but by a government replete with strong political leaders.

According to Umesao, the countries of Western Europe and Japan belonged to the first zone, and the unilinear conception of historical development was applicable only to the societies in this zone. Societies of the second zone, which constituted an enormous part of the world, followed a different historical development. Very briefly, they would travel directly from antiquity to socialist (or communist) modernity.

ZONE ONE. Antiquity ⟶ Medieval Era (feudalism) ⟶
Modernity (capitalism)
ZONE TWO. Antiquity ⟶ Modernity (socialism)

Antiquity in zone one was a copy of antiquity in zone two, but modernity in zone two was a "false form" of modernity in zone one. The dividing line between real modernity and fake modernity lay in the important point of whether or not the society had experienced a feudal-medieval period.

Thus, in the final analysis, feudalism was a precondition for genuine modernity. I have investigated the view of history inherent in Reischauer's schema of "feudalism → modernization,"[44] and within those limits Umesao and Reischauer are thoroughly consistent. Yet, on this linkage between feudalism and modernization, although Umesao's description of the actual circumstances is stronger, Reischauer explains in depth the logical links between the two conceptions to form a coherent theoretical system.

One of the main pillars of Reischauer's argument was a comparative historiographic analogy between Japanese and Chinese society. Why was it that while Japan had been responsive to the problems of modernization, China had responded sluggishly? It was not, he argued, because of a difference in historical stages between the two countries, as the Marxists suggested. One was a feudal state, the other a state where power was centralized, with qualitatively different social structures. China's advanced bureaucratic system had once been a model for European states in the period of absolutism, and the egalitarianism supporting this bureaucracy would seem a rather easy means to ensure the modernization of China. In spite of this, her lateness to modernization was due to the very state structure of China.

China's high level of civilization, Reischauer went on, gave rise to a sinocentrism because of which she disdained absorbing foreign knowledge. Her unitary, centralized power structure hampered an efficacious response to Western learning and might. The egalitarianism central to Chinese society guaranteed to the people an equality for success in life; and because of this, China retained the bureaucratic system rather than moving toward an intention-oriented ethic, as in Japan. As a result, new undertakings for wealth and fame were blocked in their development as private enterprises and tended to be fully absorbed into state enterprises. Thus, China's tardiness to modernization was not due to a low level of civilization or laggard social development, but to a state structure that had developed to a high level. This state structure can be expressed as despotism and it stood in parallel to feudalism.

Reischauer's position was not uniquely his but rather a result of the research of the American "modernization" group with which he was associated. "Modernization" theory has been analyzed in a number of publications,[45] which argue that the unfolding of "modernization" theory was fundamentally linked both directly and indirectly to America's international policies in the postwar period, particularly from the 1950s. America's policy of "containment" of the socialist countries, begun shortly after the war, included economic aid to backward countries outside the socialist camp, but this "containment" policy, they argue, ended in failure. Beginning with the birth of a new China in 1949, independence for the peoples of former colonies was achieved with tempestuous momentum.

America's economic aid plan, the critics go on, confronted this flood tide by merely sending capital goods and technology and by forging a bond between these items and the local labor power, but it was too late. American policy could not rouse the development of the self-regulating economies of the backward countries with material and technological essentials alone. Reflection on this economic aid formula led to a profoundly felt need for "regional studies" that would encompass non-economic elements, and comprehensive scholarly research was promoted by collaboration between the various disciplines of economics, history, political science, and cultural anthropology. This eventually set the tone for American foreign policy.

"Modernization" theory, linked in this overall way to "regional studies," had the political aim of guarding the newly risen states from the attractive power of the socialist camp and trying to join them to the free world. In order to promote economic growth in the newly risen states where bourgeois influence was weak, state power had to play a large role, and thus these states were liable to incline toward the socialist camp. The problem for American interests lay in what possibility existed to redirect these nations toward the capitalist camp.

The categories of "capitalism" and "socialism" in "modernization" theory that was seeking a solution to this question were not different stages of development, as Marxism argued, but two distinct forms of modernization. Modernization, as it was used, meant primarily industrialization. The development of human society was a leap from preindustrial (traditional) to industrial society, and this transition was the decisive turning point in establishing the nature of each civilized society. In this sense, "capitalism" and "socialism" were merely two discrete models of industrialization. "Modernization" theory, as so conceived, sought to encompass the various societies of the peoples of the world with a generalization based on the equivalence of modernization and industrialization. Thus, all societies were capable of reaching this stage, and it was a question of secondary importance whether they took the capitalist route or the socialist route.

Considered in this framework, "capitalism" or "socialism" become a relative issue, not the Marxist path of progress *from capitalism to socialism*. Not only this, argued the "modernization" theorists, but also from the perspective that modernization was industrialization, capitalist modernization (as the spontaneous typical course for this) gained dominance over the socialist variety. For, while in the former the individual's freedom was guaranteed, the latter was premised on an unnatural system—"totalitarianism."

Thus, while accepting the equivalence of modernization and industrialization in human society as a general rule, "modernization" theory advocated taking the capitalist route as the ideal form. Wada Haruki distinguished this view—dubbed "contemporary modernization theory"—from "classical modernization theory," which had considered "free, democratic, Western society" as the ideal. According to Wada, one difference between these two modes of thought was that the "classical" variety emerged in such underdeveloped capitalist countries as

Russia and Japan and in conjunction with the political task of overcoming backwardness, whereas "contemporary modernization theory" grew out of America's international orientation of opposition to revolution. He argued that while the former sought certain theoretical underpinnings in Marxist theory, the latter set out explicitly from a position critical of Marxism. Despite these historical differences cited by Wada, both sides clearly shared a Europocentric position.

It is evident that this conception of "modernization" theory offered high praise for Japan's modernization and was politically linked to Japan's place in American policy. And, in the academic world, there was high praise particularly for the Tokugawa feudal system and the Meiji Restoration. It is well known that "modernization" theorists produced energetic studies in this area, and these studies led to the convening of the Japan–United States Hakone Conference (August–September 1960). This event brought to our attention the commencement of a new era in American-Japanese relations following the revision of the Security Treaty. Professor Reischauer, who would subsequently become American ambassador to Japan, naturally attended the conference.

Because Reischauer's thesis was formulated and expressed with this background, he was inundated with criticism from Japanese Marxist historians. The critique went along a variety of lines, including: 1) an identification of and attack on the nature of Reischauer's thesis as the ideology of imperialism; and 2) an attack on the point that his view of history ignored the role of the people in history (in his conception of feudalism, serfdom was ignored in the definition of the feudal system).

The first argument was made by the late Horigome Yōzō in his essay, "Hōkensei saihyōka e no shiron" (A reevaluation of feudalism).[46] He called for a critical attitude toward politics and noted that the problem of the feudalism-modernization connection central to Reischauer's position was not Reischauer's own innovation but was based on a notion current in Western scholarly circles. I myself am in agreement with this last point and have attempted an investigation of Reischauer's thesis—or perhaps better referred to as an investigation of how to establish a critical position.[47] To go beyond Reischauer's thesis, or "modernization" theory itself, requires in-depth study of the conception of feudalism. In this sense, I hesitate to say if the second criticism has yet been anchored in firm scholarly work.

Reischauer did not see feudalism as a general phenomenon in world history but as a distinct social system of peoples who shared the experience of having lived under the specific conditions of feudalism. The following points enable us to say that this conception of feudalism was not Reischauer's creation alone. In 1950 a joint research project on feudal systems was carried out at Princeton University. Papers were prepared by specialists on feudalism in eight regional areas—Western Europe, Japan, China, ancient Mesopotamia and Iran, ancient Egypt, India, Byzantium, and Russia—and Reischauer was responsible for the Japan portion. The essays were edited and published by Rushton Coulborn in the volume *Feudalism in History*.[48]

In his review of the book, Masubuchi Tatsuo[49] describes Coulborn's summary presentation concerning the formation of feudalism as follows. Feudalism does not necessarily arise anywhere after the collapse of an ancient empire. It is a phenomenon seen in the marginal territories of an empire, and in the more central areas order is reestablished by following a different route. Thus, an empire is restored by a revival of the centralized bureaucratic system itself. Concrete examples of states that became feudal are Western Europe and Japan, whereas the Byzantine empire, which inherited the Roman empire, is offered as an example of a revival of an ancient empire. In China as well, we see the succession, after the collapse of the Han empire, of temporary disunion, then the Sui-T'ang empire, and then the centralized empire from the Sung onward. Indeed, there was a tendency toward regional independence for a while in the Southern Dynasties, but this was a false feudalism, merely a temporary phenomenon when seen from the overall perspective.

While commenting on Coulborn's overview, Masubuchi claims that this conceptualization was borrowed from the work of the German medievalist Otto Hinze. In Hinze's usage, "feudalism" is an irregular form in the normal historical course from clan to state and from there to despotic empire. When a young race, having just shaken free of the clan system, is swayed from this normal process of development by contact with a highly civilized empire in a state of decline, the result is feudalism, according to Hinze.

In citing feudalism as one of the two possible routes following the collapse of an ancient empire, Reischauer, Coulborn, and Hinze all agree. Furthermore, as I will discuss shortly, Karl Wittfogel's conception of feudalism is fully consistent with theirs in this regard. And what is more, it seems to me that Ishimoda Shō's notion of feudalism, as expressed in his book *Chūsei teki sekai no keisei*, and that of Katō Shigeshi from his prewar essay, "Shina to bushi kaikyū," both discussed earlier, contained very similar conceptions to these. Ishimoda later altered his approach to the two paths, so that it was two paths *toward feudalism*; and he went further to stress the common points of these two as feudal systems. But, as I have already detailed, this tendency ran into difficulties. Just when the position of unilinear development theories was beginning to be undermined, multilinear theses (which the unilinear theories intended to surmount) were taking up the very same problem of feudalism and returning it to center stage.

Conceptions of Feudalism in Western Academic Circles and China's Autocratic Society

The theoretical origins of the conception of feudalism held by "modernization" theorists were by no means superficial. As Horigome noted, they go back to Max Weber's theories. Weber's view that feudalism was a degenerated form of patrimonial bureaucracy is well known. He argued that the centralized patrimonial bureaucracy in which the sovereign concentrates power in his own hands runs into difficulty maintaining itself in pure form and thus continually tends toward a personal, status system of patrimony that offers officialdom considerable independence. The extreme form of this is feudalism, and Weber distinguishes nonhereditary *Pfründe* (beneficiary) feudalism and hereditary *Lehn* (investiture) feudalism. Although the former has not yet been able to shed its patrimonial bureaucratic attributes completely, the latter has. Thus, *Lehn* feudalism consists of a loyalty bond, as its spiritual foundation, which links a specific sovereign to a specific vassal; it is never a one-sided relationship, but rather a contractual bond between two parties. While *Pfründe* feudalism's main principle of control is the vassal's official duty (*Pietät*, piety) to the sovereign, fidelity (*Treue*) is appended to the principle of *Lehn*. As Weber put it: "*Lehn* feudalism is an extreme case of the patrimonial structure." [50]

Lehn feudalism, according to Weber, was a particular feudal system seen only in medieval Europe. Or, rather, the particular form of feudalism known as *Lehn* was distinguished when Weber inserted the historical premise that the dominant pattern that had given rise to capitalist modernity was European society. This is clear from Weber's statement about the relationship between feudalism and modern capitalism. He noted that although feudalism possessed the proclivity to obstruct the development of modern capitalism—through investment in land as property, or suppression by traditionalism, and so on— the great security that the feudal legal order held compared with the patrimonial state could provide an advantageous element for capitalist development. The opportunity for an individual to acquire property through random chance, as under the patrimonial state, disappeared. But, for that very reason, feudalism became advantageous to the establishment of the rational structure of capitalism itself.

Because in medieval Europe there was no accumulation of wealth in the dependency relations of the patrimonial state, as there was with officials and state-authorized merchants in the Orient, China, and Russia, capital flowed to purely non-official profit channels in the form of wholesale domestic industry and manufacture. Also, the more the feudal stratum shut off new wealth from playing a role in officialdom and political power, and prevented it from acquiring control over the aristocracy, the more it forced new wealth into purely urban capitalist use.

This all points to what Reischauer called intention-orientation. The opposition he set up was between feudal Japan's intention-orientation and the bureaucratic Chinese status-orientation. In Weber as well, China is cited as one of the prototypes of a patrimonial bureaucratic state together with ancient Egypt. The developed bureaucratic system was furnished with a rationality making it capable, at a glance, of passing for a modern bureaucracy. However, in matters involving its content and basic principles, it could not transcend the bounds of the traditional ruling form. In a word, it had reached the apex of the patrimonial bureaucracy. Although the *formal modernity* it possessed seemed to have complied without question with the development toward modern capitalism, in fact this made its actual compliance difficult. The reason was that the rationality that this formal modernity imitated was in essence a one-sided, top-down, false rationality that could not go beyond the patrimonial bureaucratic framework.

What separated European from non-European states was whether or not the principle of rule was truly one of loyalty, based on a contract, and hence legal. However darkly colored by what seemed to be the appearance of feudalism, however firmly recognizable the telltale signs of capitalism might seem, if the substance of this principle of rule was missing, there was neither a true feudalism nor a truly modern society. Thus, "feudalism" and "modernization" emerge as categories linked by a logical necessity, and Western European society became that historical society in which this linkage could be understood. In this sense, Western European society was what Weber had in mind.

How then did Weber understand Japanese society? My knowledge is extremely limited in this area, but I believe what I have to say to be credible. Weber argues that the basic character of *Lehn* feudalism lay in its amalgamation of personal fidelity bonds originating in the "duty" (*Pietät*) of the retainer system together with their accompanying *beneficium*. Although Japanese feudalism did have the idea of a personal retainer's "duty," it lacked the manorial lord structure of *beneficium*. For instance, what daimyos were entrusted with by the shogun was *Amt* (official position), not *Lehn* (feudal tenure). Also, the daimyo obeyed perforce the shogun's unilateral orders to change fiefs. The daimyo's retainers were not feudal servants of the *Lehn* type but *Pfründe* recipients of rice stipends. Thus, Japanese feudalism did not constitute a full-fledged *Lehn* feudal system. Nonetheless, Weber continues, a contractual .legal bond offered a much more powerful basis for nurturing individualism (in the Western sense of the word) than did China's theocracy. Although Japan had been unable to generate the spirit of capitalism from within herself, she was able to adopt foreign capitalism with comparative ease. Weber also argues that the link between *honor* and *loyalty* are found only in the Western *Lehn* feudalism and in the Japanese *Gefolgschaft* (client) feudalism.

Thus, we find in Weber's view as well that feudalism—to the extent that it is genuine—carries with it the theoretical assumption of modernization; and thus, only Western European society or its equivalent, Japanese society, was equipped with this precondition and the process resulting from it. This structure is consistent with the theoretical structure of "modernization" theory. Although the two are not identical in thought, there is no doubt that the "feudalism-modernization" thesis of "modernization" theory relies to a considerable extent on Weber's sociology.

The influence exercised by Weber's comparative historical method on historical theory today is immeasurable. It has become the theoretical fount for "modernization" theory. I would also like to show how close Weber's structure was, particularly on the issue of feudalism, to the conceptions of China of two European-born historians, Étienne Balazs and Karl Wittfogel, both of whom presented incisive analyses of Chinese society.

A Hungarian-born sinologist, Étienne Balazs (1905–1963) studied primarily the society, economy, thought, and literature of the Six Dynasties, Sui, and T'ang periods, but his many writings have a breadth of vision covering the long range of Chinese history. A number of his essays were collected in *Chinese Civilization and Bureaucracy*.[51] The central issue raised in these essays was the conditions under which China had been able to sustain an imperial government for over two thousand years from the third century B.C. into the twentieth century. Balazs was also interested in the links between traditional Chinese society and post-1949 China. He claimed that it was the bureaucracy that gave Chinese society the quality of homeostasis. In the imperial period, the structure of Chinese society was a self-sufficient agriculture at the social base and a totalitarian state administering it. State bureaucrats were scholar-officials from the gentry class. It was not landownership that bestowed social position and influence upon the gentry; nor was it the hereditary passage of position or influence.

Rather, it was the administrative control function that this group performed in society. Their becoming officials was the manifestation of this function.

In this way, the bond between the state and the self-sufficient peasant village was formed through the intermediary of the bureaucracy. Since state power was considered omnipotent, this bond produced characteristics of totalitarianism, such as a reigns of terror, repression of private entrepreneurial development, and a desire among officials to avoid responsibility. Confucianism, Balazs went on, provided the ideological means used to support this system. There were indeed movements to reject or oppose this structure. Taoism's mystical idea of a return to nature, as opposed to the political conservatism of "rationalistic" Confucianism, captured people's desire to deny contemporary realities. Often this merged with peasant rebellions to topple a dynasty.

Although these popular uprisings were tinged with revolutionary coloring, Balazs felt that they could not fundamentally negate the traditional Chinese system. Rather, they ended with a repetition of the destruction and reconstruction of the traditional system that had reproduced itself into modern times.

Only when she faced an invasion by modern European powers did China reach the stage of social revolution (in a substantive sense). Balazs, however, saw the successful modern Chinese revolution as analogous to traditional bureaucratic society. In China, he argued, where the overwhelming majority of the population were poor peasants and the formation of a bourgeois class was weak, the intellectuals replaced the bourgeoisie in leading the revolution. The party bureaucrats who, as a result of the revolution, directed Chinese socialism—Balazs called it state capitalism—were comparable to the scholar-officials of the imperial era. The economy was controlled by the power of the state; state farms, for example, he likened to farming on garrison lands in the earlier period.

Thus, Balazs considered Chinese socialism a contemporary edition of the old bureaucratic state and stressed its totalitarian flavor. He pessimistically foresaw the trend toward totalitarianism—namely, bureaucratic, technocratic state control—covering the entire world, including the advanced nations of the West as well as the backward states that had formerly been colonies.

In Balazs' understanding, the permanent quality of Chinese society revolved around the "bureaucracy." He was forced to draw the conclusion that from the inauguration of the imperial system China had never in her history experienced feudalism— at least, it had never been effectively put into practice. Balazs argued that the Chinese Communists had dispensed with Marx's original four-stage schema (Asiatic society, classical slave society, medieval feudal society, and modern capitalist society), and in its place, with a schema borrowed from "vulgar Marxism," they had become adept at calling "feudal" everything that transpired between the "slave society" of ancient China and 1949. Thus, Balazs argued, this all-inclusive "feudalism" only led to a confusion in understanding. Not that China's bureaucratic society wholly lacked feudal elements, but in his view the principal ruling class in society had remained the scholar-officials, and they were not the great landowners truly befitting the station of a feudal class.

It should be clear from this brief summary that Balazs' conception of Chinese society resembled Weber's. In fact, according to Muramatsu Yūji,[52] Balazs was heavily influenced in the theoretical area by Weber's work because he had studied sinology under Otto Franke. It is safe to say that Balazs' research on China sought to offer concrete cases for Weber's ideas about China. At the same time, he undeniably shared many points in common with the view of China offered by American "modernization" theory. If there was any difference between them, it would be that "modernization" theory pinned its policy hopes on the modernization of the peoples of the world along the lines of the "free world," whereas Balazs was apprehensive about the threat of totalitarianism hanging over the future of the world. This may reveal his European liberalism, but the two fundamentally shared in the view that understood Chinese society negatively, be it as a bureaucratic or a totalitarian state.[53]

Karl A. Wittfogel is also a sinologist in the Weberian strain. According to his own recollections, Wittfogel began his work on the distinctiveness of the hydraulic society and the state under Weber's influence in the winter of 1922–23. In 1924 he began to cite the work of both Weber and Marx.[54] His study of hydraulic society was apparently constructed by laying Weber's sociological theory and Marx's view of the Asiatic mode of production on top of each other. There is clearly no need to rehearse the famous thesis of Wittfogel's book. Here I shall select several statements concerning the issue under analysis from *Oriental Despotism*, Wittfogel's comprehensive treatment of hydraulic society.

In his "Introduction," Wittfogel describes the significance of his own research on Oriental despotic society. Studies of Oriental society flourished in the age of European absolutism, but concerns shifted to other problems in the middle of the nineteenth century, the age of industrial capitalism. Although it had been hoped that liberalism would be realized at that time, total power, far from being eliminated, expanded gradually, and this revived interest in the historical experience of despotic rule. Thus, a thorough analysis of Oriental society became necessary once again.

According to Wittfogel, Oriental society is more appropriately called "hydraulic society." Marx and Engels called it the Asiatic mode of production, and hence originally argued for a two-tracked mechanism for the development of societies. Later Marxists peddled a unilinear theory under Marx's name. A representative case would be Soviet scholars of East Asia who, for political reasons, denied the existence of an Asiatic mode of production. Thus, Wittfogel claims, they tried to conceal the bureaucratic essence of the Soviet Union's new totalitarian control—a modern edition of Oriental despotism.

Beginning with the category of "hydraulic society" (a society with irrigated agriculture under large-scale governmental direction), Wittfogel offers an analysis of the functions performed by the Oriental despotic state in every area from politics to the economy to culture. But, as is clear from this formulation, it is not only applicable to traditional Oriental society but also points toward a universal pattern covering all "totalitarian" states, be they ancient, modern, East, or West. He notes that his comparative historical analysis is based firmly in the work of American cultural anthropologists and is the result of making free use of extremely rich and widely varied sources.

The pattern of the totalitarian hydraulic state drawn by

Wittfogel shares many points in its larger framework with the views of other scholars noted earlier, such as in their discussions of China, to say the least. In describing the peculiar structure and nature of Chinese society, Wittfogel often adopts the method of comparing and contrasting it with classical antiquity and medieval Europe. Needless to say, this method is closely tied to Wittfogel's understanding of the two-tracked mechanism of world history.

What then is Wittfogel's interpretation of Japanese society? Japan, he argues, is part of the Asian mainland, and Japanese civilization bears the same traits as China and India. Furthermore, the Japanese had developed the most ingenious system of irrigated agriculture in human history. Despite all this, Japan was never hydraulic. Because of her topography, water utilization in Japan did not take an all-inclusive (hydraulic) form but rather a decentralized (hydraulic agricultural) form. It did not necessitate large-scale public works under government control, and it was administered by local managers.

These conditions for water usage, argues Wittfogel, bequeathed Japan the nature of her historical development. State policy for the establishment of a centralized bureaucracy, attempted at the time of the Taika Reforms, did not take root in Japanese society. The shift of a bureaucratic stratum into hereditary landowners and the adoption of a system of primogeniture put Japan on the road to feudalism. Medieval Japanese society was not centralized and was based on wealth. And, it was one step closer to the European feudal order than was the Chinese hydraulic pattern. The absolutist centralization of power in the hands of the government, which characterized the Edo period, was also one step closer to European absolutism, rather than an expression of Oriental despotism.

Wittfogel never denied that an Oriental character can be seen in Japanese institutions and thought. He points out that the demand for absolute obedience to the feudal lord may not be unrelated to the quasi-hydraulic nature of Japan's irrigated agriculture. Furthermore, he argues, the fact that the mode of thought of the ruling class was based on Confucianism and revered the culture of the written Chinese language is linked in one respect to the Chinese principle of a civil officialdom. In recognizing the Oriental aspect of Japanese society and simultaneously stressing its closeness to Europe, Wittfogel seems to have been influenced by Weber's conceptions.

A certain shared pattern is evident in the views of scholars who have supported a manifold structure to world history, as we have noted in these pages. They interpret world civilization by dividing it into two types centering on the feudal social system. One is the civilization that has experienced feudalism in the classical sense; the other is the civilization that has not produced it. Although the cradle of civilization of the ancient world first appeared in the latter, eventually it spread to areas on its periphery, overcame them, and finally gave birth to the feudal civilization of the former. Whereas the former followed a self-generative development toward modern capitalist society, the latter was unable to generate a further epochal evolution from the social structure of ancient civilization that had matured quite early. It was reorganized under conditions brought about by world capitalism by preserving its essence as a centralized bureaucratic society. While it may have become a colony and may have realized a socialist revolution, it could not, in either case, escape the status of a backward country. Resolution of this contradiction necessitated the reconstruction of the bureaucratic state under a new guise.

This conception of world history is based on the ideal of liberalism, a point shared by all the authors. Feudalism in their view is not simply a *form* of society, but a particular mode of human cohesion that gives rise in its pure form to a bilateral, contractual, lord-vassal bond. It overcomes the unilateral, absolutist relationship of the ancient bureaucracy and guarantees human freedom under customary law. The historical and theoretical link between feudalism and self-generating modernization can be found here. By contrast, bureaucratic society either remains ancient or pursues modernizing development through socialism—in short, "an unfree world."

This conception of world history naturally includes a critique of the unilinear development thesis of the Marxist camp. As we have seen, however, according to both Balazs and Wittfogel, originally Marx and Engels had never advocated a unilinear understanding of world history themselves. They agreed that the Asiatic mode of production and stages of European history were set up as two distinct conceptions. If this is true, then the issue of the correctness of a unilinear development theory is left unsatisfied by Marxism or bourgeois liberalism alone. The host of problems involved here will be the subject of the next section.

The Revival of the Theory of the Asiatic Mode of Production and the Problem of Feudalism

The debate over the Asiatic mode of production, which receded in the 1930s, has recaptured an international vigor over the past ten years. It has become widely known in Japan through such works as *Ajia teki seisan yōshiki no mondai* (Problems concerning the Asiatic mode of production), edited and translated by Honda Kiyoji; and *Ajia teki seisan yōshiki ronsō no fukkatsu: Sekai shi no kihon hōsoku no saikentō* (The revival of the debate over the Asiatic mode of production: A reinvestigation of the basic laws of world history), edited and translated by Fukutomi Masami.[55] I should like to discuss here how the revival of this debate is connected to the issue of feudalism, which remains the problem under analysis. The circumstances surrounding the revival of the debate have been detailed in a host of books and require no further explanation save a general description of the contours of the controversy.

The debate over the Asiatic mode of production arose in the 1920s, primarily over the problem of strategies to follow in the Chinese revolution. With the Leningrad Conference of 1931, Soviet scholars tended to deny theoretically as well as from the historical evidence that Marx's conception of the Asiatic mode rendered it a separate mode of production. Examples from the past stipulated as the Asiatic mode were now considered Asiatic forms of feudalism; and the theory that the social structure of slavery had existed in ancient Asia as well now became quite influential.

The denial of the notion of the Asiatic mode was not necessarily the result of scholarly investigation but reflected potent political objectives. Under Stalin's personal directive, theorists of the Asiatic mode were labeled Trotskyists. With this background, Stalin published in 1939 his "Dialectical and Historical Materialism," in which he stated as a law that human history traveled through five stages: primitive communism, slavery, feudalism, capitalism, and socialism. Thus, if historical facts failed to comply with this formula, the facts were deemed anomalous. This dogmatism, which stressed the formula over the facts, constituted the system of world history in the socialist camp with the political support of Stalinism.

Not until the early 1950s was this officially authorized system torn down. The "thaw" over the issue of the Asiatic mode in the Soviet Union actually began in the 1960s. As is well known, the issue was raised again by French Marxist historians at this juncture: in 1964–65, the journal *La Pensée* ran special numbers devoted to the "Asiatic mode of production." Another indication of this change in circumstance occurred at the same time with the publication of *Ocherki po problemam politekonomii kapitalizma* (Outlines of political and economic problems of capitalism) by the Soviet economist Eugen Varga.[56] In this book, Varga indicted the history that had obliterated the Asiatic mode of production from discussion and proclaimed that the time had come to restore the reputation befitting this theory.

At the end of 1964, a debate over the Asiatic mode was begun in the various institutes under the umbrella of the Soviet Academy of Sciences. Noteworthy is that the areas debated concerned not only the investigation of concepts but also of problems involving the structural formation of societies and the periodization of world history, as well as many other questions of basic theory. This entailed a reexamination of the image of world history provided by Stalin's formula, and here the problem of feudalism in Asian society came into focus. I should like to look now at the issues that emerged in the process of this debate, with the aid of the collections of translations by Honda and Fukotomi cited earlier in this section.

Jean Chesneaux, a French Marxist who played an important role in reopening the debate, cited three essential elements as practical incentives for returning serious attention to the Asiatic mode of production.[57] They were: (1) the world-historical events of the liberation of the peoples of Asian and African countries after the Second World War and their actual political and social development; (2) the spectacular advances in recent knowledge of the history of the non-European world; and (3) the emergence of the need for a theoretical battle against Marxist apostates and revisionists—Wittfogel was mentioned as a representative example. I shall examine below how these three were linked. In sum, the appearance of such a state of affairs was sufficient inducement to reinstate investigation of the Asiatic mode as the basis for penetrating research into the history of the non-European world.

Concretely, this state of affairs raised scholarly problems, such as the following: "Classical Marxist concepts, particularly those of slavery and feudalism, may not necessarily be fully applicable in the efforts to analyze non-European societies or at least certain elements in them." [58] Chesneaux raised the cases of Africa, India, Vietnam, and ancient Egypt as regions already of awakened to this sort of reexamination; and he introduced with high praise the work of the Hungarian sinologist Ferenc Tökei, *Sur le mode de production asiatique*. [59] Tökei argued the existence of the Asiatic mode in Chou dynasty China. Chesneaux was thoroughly dissatisfied with the way contemporary China interpreted her own history. "They look simplistically for the same stages in Chinese history as in European history, with feudalism following slavery. The distinctive East Asian qualities of slave or feudal society are not addressed. Not one basic fact comparable to the existence of a distinctive Mandarin state bureaucracy has been the subject of a really penetrating independent analysis." [60] Chesneaux's evaluation is liable to oversimplify the trends among Chinese historians, but he stated his position on this issue rather clearly here.

When we assign a stage for the Asiatic mode of production to a specific civilized society, then what is to be foreseen in the history of these societies as a whole? This leads to complications and difficulties inconceivable under Stalin's unilinear theory. There is the danger, of which Chesneaux was aware, that the Asiatic mode will be linked to the notion of stagnation. In order to overcome this fear, he had to clarify the stage into which the Asiatic mode would evolve. Chesneaux predicted the possibility of a course from the Asiatic mode of production to a feudal mode of production. He defined the Asiatic mode as: "the combination of the productive activities of the village communities with the economic participation of state authority which simultaneously controlled these communities and exploited them." [61] He argued that the evolution from this social structure to the feudal stage may be achieved by the expansion of private ownership of the land, and he devoted his attention with respect to China to the development of private landholding from the Han dynasty.

Chesneaux, however, did not have full confidence in this course. He argued that although Asian societies have headed toward a kind of feudalism, it could not produce anything except the sprouts of capitalism, and this feudalism (whether "genuine" or not) soon withered away. Thus, as Tökei and others noted, until the invasion of European capitalism in the nineteenth century, the various Asian societies essentially held firm in their perpetuity.

This skeptical statement implied that Chesneaux did not firmly believe in the notion of an evolution from the Asiatic to the feudal mode. Chesneaux's basic intent, as he stressed time and again, was not to raise any conclusive arguments in a hasty fashion, but to appeal for the need to develop overall research inquiries liberated from the formulaic dogmatism of the past and based upon new, contemporary knowledge. In place of the dogmatism of the universality of slavery and feudalism, he asserted, we must not bring forth a new dogmatism of the universality of the Asiatic mode of production.

One member of the group that participated with Chesneaux in the revival of discussion concerning the Asiatic mode of production was Roger Garaudy. His book, *Le problème chinois*,[62] also rejected the "dogmatic schema" that all human societies passed through the five stages of primitive communism, slavery, feudalism, capitalism, and socialism; and he claimed that China had never experienced the slave mode of production. The prototypical slave system, he argued, flourished only in Mediterranean civilizations, whereas in China, as Tökei and others had noted, the Asiatic mode of production dominated society in the Shang-Chou period. From the Han dynasty on, the Asiatic mode in its prototypical form had ceased to exist, because the lack of private ownership (one of the basic features of this mode of production) disappeared owing to the privatization of land and the accumulation of slaves. After the Asiatic mode, the feudal mode of production arrived, but it was stamped with the remnants of the Asiatic mode and bequeathed a distinctiveness to Chinese feudalism.

Hence, Chinese feudal ownership in land, in Garaudy's view, was tied to the special privileges of the imperial bureaucrats, a sort of bureaucratic feudalism. It differed immensely from the "pure feudalism" (of Europe) where the feudal lord was a direct recipient of rent paid in labor; and where all state functions, such as the military and the judicial system, were provided. The transition to capitalism that European feudalism achieved by inheriting the commodity economy of classical slavery could not be brought about with this kind of feudalism. Sprouts of capitalism, cropping up here and there, could not avoid a stage of mercantilism under state control. Rich merchants, intent on entering the official class, made the formation of a bourgeois class impossible.

In the final analysis, Garaudy's view was able to synthesize the schema of the Asiatic mode of production leading to a distinctive Chinese feudalism. As noted previously, he did not see this "feudalism" developing into modern capitalism—in this regard, he shared elements with various comparative historians who were of a liberal bent.

A free expression of views not confined to old models can be seen in the debate among Soviet historians that was touched off by the new arguments in France. According to L.V. Danilova's summary[63] of the disputation in the Institute of Philosophy of the Soviet Academy of Sciences, many theoretical issues (far beyond expectations) were raised at the symposium inaugurated by an investigation of Varga's work, such as issues concerning social structure and the periodization of world history. The relationship between the concept of the Asiatic mode of production and Marx, as well as the validity of this concept, were considered; and two opposing viewpoints emerged over whether to take the concept seriously. This issue was naturally linked to the problem of the structures of class societies.

One view strongly put forward was that the earlier official theory (slavery → feudalism → capitalism) failed to accord with the realities of the vast majority of the peoples of the world—although they had known slavery as a form of exploitation, they had not experienced it in the structural form of slavery. This view vigorously repudiated the earlier official theory that had disavowed the concept of the Asiatic mode and recognized the existence of a slave stage in various non-European regions. This not only involved an interpretation of Asian history but was also tied to a systematic understanding of world history.

There was also the view that the unilinear development theory was applicable only in the Mediterranean world and was doubtful for the whole of mankind. Of course, there were opposing arguments, but, as Danilova noted, the need for a reinvestigation of the three-stage periodization that had previously been taken for granted was affirmed by the majority of participants.

The contested points expanded to include problems of early class societies as well as methodological issues. The latter in particular gave rise to a view that sought to underline geography as a constituent element of productive capacity and a basis for simplistic developmental theories. Another position that became the object of argumentation saw the role played by the state in the later primitive period as achieving the function of organizer of social production, rather than as the instrument of violence for class rule. In this view can be seen an argument indicating the transition from a theory of slavery to one of the Asiatic mode of production. This also pointed to a revival of general interest in theories of the state.

Thus, the reopening of the debate on the Asiatic mode of production in the Soviet Union led to a recognition of the need for a reexamination of the established concepts concerning the development of human history. Summarizing their work, including that of the Chesneaux and the French Marxists, Soviet historians cast grave doubts on the earlier unilinear theory of development. As noted previously, the critique of the unilinear Marxist theory first raised in the liberal camp by American "modernization" theorists eventually caught fire within the Marxist camp as well. Despite their ideological differences, both sides shared a certain common objective.

What happened to bring this about? Perhaps Chesneaux's statement, cited earlier, is suggestive here. He pointed to the actual liberation and development of the peoples of non-European, underdeveloped nations after the Second World War as the first occasion for the revival of the debate on the Asiatic mode. If Marxism proved truly incapable of grasping the realities of world history, Chesneaux argued, then this was nothing short of self-immolation for Marxism. These new realities, with the strains they imposed on theory, worked the same way on the liberal camp, whose main force was in America. Without a theoretical grasp of these realities, decisions on world policy were impossible.

The question of how to go about understanding the historical structure of these newly risen peoples, considered the "casting vote" for contemporary world history, formed one aspect of the competitive struggle between the two camps. As one of the motives for the revival of debate on the Asiatic mode, Chesneaux pointed to the need for an unmitigated theoretical struggle against Marxist renegades and revisionists. This problem was not only for "defectors" from Marxism, however, for it could equally be applied to the entire ideology of the liberal camp.

In any case, the belatedness of the Marxists was clearly undeniable. There was a discrepancy of five to ten years, for example, between the formulation of "modernization" theory and the rehabilitation of the theory of the Asiatic mode of production. In terms of theoretical content as well, the former distinguished Europe (and Japan) from the non-European world, and offered a multilinear system of world history, while the latter, perhaps saving its strength for the battle with dogmatism, remained far from systematization. A more essential question, however, has not been mentioned. The intellectual origins of the former lay in a modernism whose main feature was industrialization, as pointed out earlier. Thus, the real issue for the latter was from what stance to confront "modernization" theory and put together a new system of world history that began with a revival of the Asiatic mode debate. Hence, it also seemed necessary that the problem of feudalism be more deeply understood in this regard.

Four

Concluding Remarks

I am not a specialist in the problem of feudalism in history. The history of research into this issue, as I have described it, merely represents my own reordering of the problems that have caught my eye. But it seems to me clear, even within the narrow range of my own knowledge, that the issue of feudalism in non-European societies cannot be overlooked as if it were something self-evident. It has not at all been firmly established that these societies went through feudalism. In the case of China, for example, we have seen the perspective that takes the concept of bureaucracy as more useful than the category of feudalism. We have also noted the suggestion that, even if the feudal stage was experienced, one should assume that this was something far removed from Western feudalism. In short, the issue of feudalism in Asia, as well as in China, has now reverted to the state of being an unknown entity.

The first cause of this reversion—namely, the rise of non-European peoples—need not be repeated. When we look squarely at this new reality, we can no longer close the door on the history of these people with categories drawn from European history. We need a new methodology to comprehend from within the histories of each of these individual peoples.

The officially sanctioned historical materialist theory, which for over thirty years reigned in the Marxist camp, was merely a dogma unconscious of this new reality, and this fact increasingly began to dawn on a good many people. The reason was that the more they applied the official formula to the histories of the non-European world, the more difficulties they encountered and the greater the dilemma they faced of lacking the evidence to fit the formula. This was sharply sensed also in Japan's postwar experience.

However, the "modernization" school's pedigree has proven unsatisfactory as well. While theoretically trying to understand the non-European world in its essence, it remains merely a Western-centered interpretation. As a projection of an image of the European world, the non-European world has been burdened with the role of heightening the value of the former. This lays bare the nature of "modernization" theory as a new colonialist view of world history.

Be that as it may, we find ourselves in a situation necessitating a return to the dimensions of the unknown and a pursual of an investigation of this issue in Chinese history. Where in the world is it best to begin the unraveling of this difficult problem? Before bringing this chapter to a close, I must briefly consider this point, but first let me insert into the analysis an article by Sakai Kakusaburō, "Hōken shakai no kōzō: Chūgoku hokensei no kentō kara hōken shakai e no ippan riron e" (The structure of feudal society: From an investigation of Chinese feudalism to a general theory of feudal society).[64] While concerned to a certain extent with the problems we have been examining, this essay seems to raise perspectives not previously considered.

Sakai argues as follows. What allowed the establishment of a theory of modernization as a reproduction of the notion of Asian stagnation was, in addition to Japan's and the West's success in modernizing, a reductionism to the lowest common denominator without a theory sufficient to coordinate studies of Asian feudal societies with those of Japanese and European societies. In other words, studies of Asian history since the war generalized feudalism as landlord control over the peasantry and claimed that feudalism had been experienced in Asia as well, but the connection between the base and the superstructure was never clarified. The problem was never resolved as to why the same base might give birth to a different superstructure. Or, on the contrary, feudalism in the Chou dynasty was argued to be fundamentally different from Western European feudalism, but no explanation was given for why they produced similar political systems. These issues reveal the theoretical lacunae in postwar conceptions of feudalism.

With this premise, Sakai discusses the structural features of feudal society and then proceeds with an analysis of Chinese society. He argues that the decisive structural characteristics of feudal society are the organization of a stratum of territorial lords, regional states, and a political framework that is decentralized into segments and strata. The society is run by a status system of rank and occupation, based on birth, and at the highest rung dwells a military aristocracy that dominates military power. This structure is bequeathed to subsequent generations by a system of single inheritance and is maintained by a systematic religion as a unifying spiritual principle.

If we look at these features from the perspective of a system of ownership, Sakai argues, it was characterized by the lack of a completely exclusive system of ownership and had an incomplete, open form of ownership layered in several strata. The stratified structure of feudal power was based on these layers— for example, in comparing Japan with the West, the extraordinary centralization of power in the former was due to the strength of its level of completeness. A society at the opposite end of the spectrum from feudal society (with this incomplete ownership system) would be a society where the system of ownership is complete. Its organization would be *Gesellschaft* and bureaucratic; and the state would assume a centralized form or a form lacking a government. Hence, these two types of societies flow into each other.

If we adopt this model to the historical materialist theory of stages of development, then the incomplete ownership system can emerge in two periods: (1) the transition from primitive society to slavery where a system of ownership is complete; and (2) the decline of slavery, namely a period when overlapping (common) property exists between classes because while slaves are recovering ownership rights, it is not yet a complete system of private property. Chou feudalism, for example, is a case of feudal society preceding slavery, and feudalism (serf society), in the theory of stages of development, is a product of this second period.

Looking at the problem in this way, feudalism can never be a system formed simply under prescribed conditions. Sakai proposes the early Ming as a society furnished with the features of feudalism. After the collapse of the Chou feudal system, feudalism did not take shape as a structure extending throughout Chinese society. However, partial lord-vassal bonds continued to exist over the ages in the form of a system of feudal titles, which developed particularly from the late Jurchen-Chin era, through the Yüan and Ming, and into the early Ch'ing. The Ming especially enfeoffed members of the imperial family and meritorious officials and bestowed titular rank and manors (*lu-t'ien*).[65] These manors were often converted into official "aristocratic estates" (*chuang-t'ien*).[66] Those who received titular rank generally held hereditary military posts, and the troops under them were organized into military households through a system of heredity. According to Sakai, the Yüan dynasty was an era of decline for slavery; in the Chin-Yüan transition years, the Sung and Chin bureaucratic strata were destroyed, and a military class as the new rulers emerged to form the kind of feudalism described earlier.

Hence, Sakai lays greater emphasis on the break between Sung and Yüan than between T'ang and Sung, but this does not mean that such feudal ties covered the entirety of Chinese society. There was a middle class of self-managing peasants, he argues, who simultaneously owned land and were under state control as direct producers. Since this middle class embodied in itself feudal relations of production, its dissolution gave rise to feudal bonds; however, the two classes that composed the feudal bond were becoming a middle class owing to upward and downward mobility. In this way, feudalism and bureaucracy flowed into each other. Also, bureaucracy stifled feudal rule and led to a system of centralized power, and this gave rise to an indirect bond whereby the class of feudal lords controlled the middle class through the mechanism of the state. And, a tendency ensued toward the bureaucratization of the feudal lords.

The preceding points, although extremely general, summarize Sakai's argument. Because his category of an "incomplete system of ownership" provides a logic sufficient to explain the correspondence between the base and the superstructure of feudal society, his effort to describe in general terms the stages of world history is worthy of our attention. So far as concerns an interpretation of Chinese history, however, one is hard-pressed to say that he has been completely successful. His intention was to overcome the understanding of Asia offered by "modernization" theory by proving the existence of feudalism in Chinese history. Hence, he tried to locate in the Ming the most feudal period in Chinese history, but, as he himself put it, this feudal system was only partial in that it never covered all of Chinese society structurally and was largely limited by the bureaucratic system. Thus, the question to answer is: How is one to approach this bureaucratic society? Since he cannot overestimate the feudal relations in Chinese society, this very question becomes the flip side of his original aim.

One further difficulty is related to this issue. The reason "modernization" theory stresses the stage of feudalism is in order to show that feudalism prepared the logic internally for modern society. While the bilateral, contractual, personal bond that characterized the feudal lord-vassal bond in Europe accompanied a system of status, it also guaranteed mutual rights. Without the guarantee of these rights, the establishment of modern society was considered impossible. Aside from Western Europe, only Japan had undergone a feudal system of this sort; when a feudal political structure seemed to have been spotted in regions other than these, because it was deemed false feudalism it could not be equated with Western European feudalism. In other words, the difference between real and bogus feudalism hinged on the ethos that supported a given system—this seemed to be the position of "modernization" theory with one of its origins in Weber. Thus, Sakai should have contemplated this issue if he sought to overcome "modernization" theory. His theory of feudalism, however, remained primarily a general theory of construction that ignored this point.

The clue to the problem under analysis is uncovered at the very point where Sakai's effort falls short. In reconsidering the importance of Western feudalism, the fact that it formed the premise for modern society and the fact that the ancient European world was transcended by it seem to be intimately related. Medieval society was formed by destroying the ancient society of public law based on blood ties and by creating a new personal universe of private law and of the self.

In Europe this epochal transformation was apparently realized by "feudalism." In other words, "feudalism" connoted the European form by which the ancient world was sublated. If this perception of the issue is acceptable, then clearly we must not limit ourselves simply to whether or not the political system or structure of feudalism existed when we trace the historical evolution of traditional Asian societies. Previous experience has taught us that the thesis of Asian stagnation originated precisely by limiting the problem in this way. However, the perspective that takes the universal nature of feudalism to be simply serfdom, as was the economic base of Western European feudalism, linked tightly to a decentralized superstructure, and which then locates this system in the various societies of Asia is hard to accept as a method for understanding traditional Asian societies.

To make a proper comparison with Europe inherently requires a search in the societies of Asia to see: (1) how the ancient world—namely, the history from the distant past which formed the origins of world civilization—was transcended; and (2) by what process and in what modes the formation of the medieval world took shape. In a word, it requires a consideration of the "meaning" of feudalism in European history in the context of Asian history.

As we have seen thus far, many scholars have pointed to the bureaucracy as the distinctive feature of traditional Chinese society. This is not mistaken in and of itself. However, few people indeed can deny that there has been a historical development within the "perpetual and unchanging" framework of bureaucratic society. Thus, the problem is not to focus solely on the framework and ask if it is bureaucratic or feudal (let alone falsely or genuinely feudal), but to investigate the structure of the individual development of each society that falls within the bureaucratic framework. It is only natural that bureaucracy did not emerge solely by itself but had a social base that propped it up. Bureaucracy as the edifice together with its foundations existed both in a mutually supportive relationship and in positions mutually opposed. If we can actually prove that the dialectic between the two relationships caused traditional Asian society to move from ancient to medieval times, then would this not lend credence to the possibility that the capacity for self-development would create Asia's distinctive modernity, a modernity that could not be identified with Europe's modernity?

Glossary to Part I

Notes to Part I

(All publishers are located in Tokyo unless otherwise noted.)

1. 石母田正,「中世的世界の形成」. First published by Itō shoten, 1946; later revised and reprinted by Tokyo University Press, 1957.

2. *Ritsuryō* 律令. These were the penal (*ritsu*) and administrative (*ryō*) provisions in the legal codes of the Taihō Code of 701. They were patterned largely on the model of the T'ang code. (JAF)

3. Watanabe Yoshimichi 渡部義通, *Kodai shakai no kōzō* 古代社会の 構造 (The structure of ancient society), Itō shoten, 1948; later republished by San'ichi shobō.

4. Katō Shigeshi 加藤繁, "Shina to bushi kaikyū" 支那と武士階級 (China and the warrior class), *Shigaku zasshi* 史学雑誌 50.1 (January 1939), pp. 1–19.

5. *Hsieh-tou* 械闘. See Kitamura Hironao 北村敬直, "Shindai kaitō no ichi kōsatsu" 清代械闘の一考察 (A study of clan feuds in the Ch'ing), *Shirin* 史林 33.1 (January 1950), pp. 64–77. (JAF)

6. 「中世史研究の起点: 封建制への二つの道について」, in *Nihon shi kenkyū nyūmon* 日本史研究入門 (Introduction to the study of Japanese history), edited by Tōyama Shigeki 遠山茂樹, Tokyo University Press, 1949; later reprinted in Ishimoda's *Chūsei teki sekai no keisei*, cited in note 1.

7. *Kinsei* 近世, so as to distinguish it from *kindai* 近代 or modern. (JAF)

8. "Hōkensei seiritsu no tokushitsu ni tsuite" 封建制成立の特質につ いて (On the nature of the establishment of feudalism), *Shisō* 思想 302 (August 1949), pp. 1–17.

9. In his essay, "Kiki ni okeru rekishigaku no kadai" 危機における 歴史学の課題 (Historiographic issues in crisis), in *Rekishi to minzoku no hakken* 歴史と民族の発見 (The discovery of history and ethnicity), Tokyo University Press, 1952, vol. 1, pp. 3–51, Ishimoda discussed the importance of arranging the issues in roughly the following way. The debate over the Asiatic mode of production, set off by strategic problems of the Chinese revolution of the 1920s, had considerable historiographic importance in that it raised in a broad manner theoretical problems concerning the distinctiveness of Asia. The debate in Japan, however, being removed from the actual problems given rise to by the Chinese revolution, became a scholarly, intellectual discussion. This spawned a tendency not to study the bitter popular struggles that had pushed forward the history of Asian peoples, who at a glance appeared stagnant over the preceding two thousand years, and to comprehend the realities of Asia with the simple magic formula of "Asiatic stagnation." It seemed like attention was then concentrated on the reasons why this "stagnation" had come about. Not only was the theory that had been assigned the task of destroying "Asiatic stagnation" dragged unawares into the theory supporting it—namely, the theory of imperialism's control over Asia—but it also became a rationale for Asian peoples' lethargy and inactivity, and a groundless reason for glorifying Western Europe. Additionally, it was linked to a despair for the masses of Asia,

and so on. Thus, the problem of overcoming the theory of stagnation was raised poignantly within the Marxist camp as a theoretical issue.

10. 前田直典,「東アジアに於ける古代の終末」, in *Chūgoku shi no jidai kubun* 中国史の時代区分 (Periodization in Chinese history), edited by Suzuki Shun 鈴木俊 and Nishijima Sadao 西嶋定生, Tokyo University Press, 1957, pp. 349–367; included in Maeda, *Genchō shi no kenkyū* 元朝史の研究 (Studies in Yüan history), Tokyo University Press, 1973, pp. 205–221.

11. 松本新八郎,「原始・古代社会における基本的矛盾について」, in *Sekai shi no kihon hōsoku* 世界史の基本法則 (The fundamental laws of world history), edited by the Rekishigaku kenkyūkai 歴史学研究会, Iwanami shoten, 1949, pp. 2–35.

12. 西嶋定生,「古代国家の権力構造」, in *Kokka kenryoku no shodankai* 国家権力の諸段階 (The stages of state power), edited by the Rekishigaku kenkyūkai, Iwanami shoten, 1950, pp. 1–24.

13. 堀敏一,「中国における封建国家の形態」, in ibid., pp. 59–67.

14. Nagahara Keiji's 永原慶二 paper was entitled "Nihon ni okeru hōken kokka no keitai" 日本における封建国家の形態 (Forms of the feudal state in Japan).

15. According to Tōyama Shigeki, although Hori's paper at that time included a critique of Ishimoda's idea of the "two paths to feudalism," Nagahara's and Ishimoda's papers at this conference offered no response to the criticism. See Tōyama, *Sengo no rekishigaku to rekishi ishiki* 戦後の歴史学と歴史意識 (Historiography and historical consciousness in the postwar period), Iwanami shoten, 1968, pp. 68–89. Although this difference of viewpoints existed between Hori and Ishimoda at the time, I believe that, generally speaking, their positions complemented each other in establishing a theory of Chinese feudalism.

16. *Chia-t'ien* 假田. A system whereby produce was remitted from land leased with usufructuary rights. See Hoshi Ayao 星斌夫, *Chūgoku shakai keizai shi goi* 中国社会経済史語彙 (Dictionary of Chinese social and economic history), Tōyō bunko, 1966, p. 32. (JAF)

17. "Kandai ni okeru kokka zaisei to teishitsu zaisei to no kubetsu narabi ni teishitsu ippan" 漢代に於ける国家財政と帝室財政との区別並に帝室一斑 (The distinction between state finances and imperial household finances in the Han dynasty, and a look at the imperial household), in *Shina keizai shi kōshō* 支那経済史考証 (Textual studies in Chinese economic history), Tōyō bunko, 1952, vol. 1, pp. 35–156.

18. *Chan-t'ien* 占田 and *k'e-t'ien* 課田 were both parts of the land-tax law instituted by Ssu-ma Yen 司馬炎 (Chin Wu-ti 晋武帝, r. 265–290), founder of the Western Chin. *Chan-t'ien* was a rule applying to free peasants and allowed 70 *mou* of land to each family head and 30 *mou* to each of their wives. *K'e-t'ien* was a rule applying to government-controlled lands, according to which all registered adults (ages 16 to 60) had the right to 50 *mou* for men and 20 *mou* for women; and all registered males (ages 13 to 16 or 60 to 65) received half a share. See Kawakatsu Yoshio 川勝義雄, *Gi-Shin-Nambokuchō: Sōdai na bunretsu jidai* 魏晋南北朝：壮大な分裂時代 (Wei, Chin, Northern and Southern Dynasties: An era of great disunity), Kōdansha, 1974, pp. 140–144. (JAF)

19. Nishijima Sadao, "Tengai no kanata" 碾磑の彼方 (The background of the stone mill), *Rekishigaku kenkyū* 歴史学研究 125 (January 1947), pp. 38–46; [expanded and] included in Nishijima, *Chūgoku keizaishi kenkyū* 中国経済史研究 (Studies in Chinese economic history), Tokyo University Press, 1966, pp. 235–278.

20.「唐末諸叛乱の性格」, *Tōyō bunka* 東洋文化 7 (November 1951), pp. 52–94.

21. In Japan it was the heads of the military houses, in Germany the power of the king, according to Hori.

22.「黄巣の叛乱：唐末変革期の一考察」, *Tōyō bunka kenkyūjo kiyō* 東洋文化研究所紀要 13 (November 1957), pp. 1–108.

23.「藩鎮親衛軍の権力構造」, in ibid. 20 (March 1960), pp. 75–147.

24. "Tōmatsu no henkaku to nōminsō no bunkai" 唐末の変革と農民層の分解 (The changes of the late T'ang and the dissolution of the peasantry), *Rekishi hyōron* 歴史評論 88 (September 1957), pp. 2–12.

25. 仁井田陞,「中国社会の『封建』とフューダリズム」, *Tōyō bunka* 5 (April 1951), pp. 1–39; [revised and] included in Niida Noboru, *Chūgoku hōsei shi kenkyū* 中国法制史研究 (Studies in Chinese legal history), vol. 3, *Dorei nōdo hō, kazoku sonraku hō* 奴隷農奴法・家族村落法 (Laws governing slavery and serfdom, laws governing the family and the village), Tokyo University Press, 1962, pp. 97–146.

26. Tanigawa does not list the writings of Sudō here. The work by Sudō which Niida cites in this connection include: (a) "Sōdai no denkosei" 宋代の佃戸制 (The tenancy system of the Sung dynasty), *Rekishigaku kenkyū* 143 (January 1950), pp. 20–40; and (b) *Sōdai kanryōsei to dai tochi shoyū* 宋代官僚制と大土地所有 (The Sung bureaucracy and large landownership), vol. 12 in the series: *Shakai kōsei shi taikei* 社会構成史体系 (Series on the history of societal formations), Nihon hyōronsha, 1950. (JAF)

27. *Chūgoku hōsei shi kenkyū*, p. 97.

28. Ibid., p. 98, emphasis added by Tanigawa. (JAF)

29.「中国の同族又は村落の土地所有問題」, in ibid., pp. 683–740.

30. Taga Akigorō 多賀秋五郎, *Sōfu no kenkyū, shiryōhen* 宗譜の研究 資料編 (A study of clan genealogies, section on sources), Tōyō bunko, 1960.

31. *Chūgoku hōsei shi kenkyū*, p. 687, emphasis added by Tanigawa. (JAF)

32. Miyazaki Ichisada 宮崎市定, "Sōdai igo no tochi shoyū keitai" 宋代以後の土地所有形体 (Forms of landownership from the Sung dynasty onward), *Tōyōshi kenkyū* 東洋史研究 12.2 (December 1952), pp. 1–34; included in his *Ajia shi kenkyū* アジア史研究 (Studies in Asian history), vol. 4, Kyoto, Tōyōshi kenkyūkai, 1974, pp. 87–129.

33. See, for example, Kusano Yasushi 草野靖, "Dai tochi shoyū to denkosei no tenkai" 大土地所有と佃戸制の展開 (Large landholding and the development of tenancy), in *Iwanami kōza sekai rekishi 9: Chūsei 3* 岩波講座世界歴史 9：中世 3 (Iwanami's history of the world 9: Medieval 3), Iwanami shoten, 1970, pp. 345–382; Oyama Masaaki 小山正明, "Ajia no hōkensei: Chūgoku hōkensei no mondai" アジアの封建制：中国封建制の問題 (Asian feudalism: The problem of Chinese feudalism), in *Gendai rekishigaku no seika to kadai 2: kyōdōtai, doreisei, hōkensei* 現代歴史学の成果と課題 2：共同体・奴隷制・封建制 (Results and issues in contemporary historiography 2: "community," slavery, feudalism), Aoki shoten, 1974, pp. 119–136.

34. See Hori Toshikazu, "Tō teikoku no hōkai" 唐帝国の崩壊 (The collapse of the T'ang empire), in *Kodai shi kōza 10: Sekai teikoku no shomondai* 古代史講座 10：世界帝国の諸問題 (Symposium on ancient history 10: Problems of world empire), Gakuseisha, 1964, pp. 236–270; and Oyama, "Ajia no hōkensei."

35. 柳田節子,「郷村制の展開」, in *Iwanami kōza sekai rekishi 9: Chūsei 3*, pp. 309–344.

36. *Liang-shui hu* 両税戸.

37. Hori, "Kindensei no seiritsu" 均田制の成立 (The formation of the equal field system), 2 parts, *Tōyōshi kenkyū* 24.1 (June 1965), pp. 30–53; 24.2 (September 1965), pp. 51–67; and "Chūgoku kodai shi to kyōdōtai no mondai"

中国古代史と共同体の問題 (Ancient Chinese history and the issue of "community"), *Sundai shigaku* 駿台史学 27 (September 1970), pp. 162–183. The former of these essays appears in a revised and much expanded form in Hori's *Kindensei no kenkyū* 均田制の研究 (Studies of the equal field system), Iwanami shoten, 1975. The latter essay is included in *Gendai rekishigaku no kadai* 現代歴史学の課題 (Problems of contemporary historiography), Aoki shoten, 1971.

38. Roughly, a Japanese way of saying: "It's time to start afresh." (JAF)

39. "Rikuchō kizokusei shakai no shiteki seikaku to ritsuryō taisei e no tenkai" 六朝貴族制社会の史的性格と律令体制への展開 (The historical character of society under the Six Dynasties aristocratic system and the evolution of a legal order), *Shakai keizai shigaku* 社会経済史学 31.1–5 (1966), pp. 204–225; included in Tanigawa, *Chūgoku chūsei shakai to kyōdōtai* 中国中世社会と共同体 (Medieval Chinese society and "community"), Kokusho kankōkai, 1976, pp. 147–173.

40. 梅棹忠夫,「文明の生態史観序説」, *Chūō kōron* 中央公論 72.2 (February 1957), pp. 32–49.

41. 『日本近代化の新しい見方』, Kōdansha gendai shinsho, 1965. This volume did not appear in English. It is a collection of Reischauer's essays and conversations, most of which appeared individually in Japanese language publications. (JAF)

42. "Chūgoku shi kenkyū no atarashii kadai: Hōkensei no saihyōka mondai ni furete" 中国史研究の新しい課題：封建制の再評価問題にふれて (A new problem in the study of Chinese history: On the reevaluation of feudalism), *Nihon shi kenkyū* 日本史研究 94 (November 1967), pp. 8–24; included in Tanigawa, *Chūgoku chūsei shakai to kyōdōtai*, pp. 174–197.

43. Ueyama Shumpei 上山春平, "Rekishikan no mosaku" 歴史観の模索 (Search for a view of history), *Shisō no kagaku* 思想の科学 1.1 (January 1959), pp. 27–39; included in *Dai Tō-A sensō no imi* 大東亜戦争の意味 (The meaning of the great war in East Asia), Chūō kōron sha, 1964, vol. 1, pp. 162–178.

44. See Tanigawa essay cited in note 42.

45. Wada Haruki 和田春樹, "Gendai teki 'kindaika' ron no shisō to ronri" 現代的近代化論の思想と論理 (The thought and logic of contemporary "modernization" theory), *Rekishigaku kenkyū* 318 (November 1966), pp. 2–12; Kimbara Samon 金原左門, *"Nihon kindaika" ron no rekishizō* ,日本近代化論の歴史像 (The historical image of "Japanese modernization" theory), Chūō University Press, 1968; and Miyamoto Mataji 宮本又次, editor, *Amerika no Nihon kenkyū* アメリカの日本研究 (Japanology in America), Tōyō keizai shimpō sha, 1970.

46. Horigome Yōzō 堀米庸三,「封建制再評価への試論」, *Tembō* 展望 87.3 (March 1966), pp. 16–49; included in *Rekishi no imi* 歴史の意味 (The meaning of history), Chūō kōron sha, 1970, pp. 146–208.

47. See Tanigawa essay cited in note 42.

48. Rushton Coulborn, editor, *Feudalism in History*, Princeton, N.J., Princeton University Press, 1956. Reischauer's essay appears on pp. 26–48.

49. 増淵龍夫, "Rekishi ni okeru ruiji to hikaku no imi: Kūrubōn hencho *Rekishi ni okeru hōkensei* o yonde" 歴史における類似と比較の意味：クールボーン編著『歴史における封建制』を読んで (The meaning of analogy and comparison in history: On reading *Feudalism in History*, edited by Coulborn), *Shisō* 思想 412 (October 1958), pp. 1–14.

50. Japanese translation of Weber's *The Sociology of Control* by Sera Terushirō 世良晃志郎, *Shihai no shakaigaku* 支配の社会学, Sōbunsha, 1962, vol. 2, p. 289.

51. Japanese translation: *Chūgoku bummei to kanryōsei* 中国文明と官僚制, by Muramatsu Yūji 村松祐次, Misuzu shobō, 1971. (English translation by H. M. Wright, New Haven and London, Yale University Press, 1964—JAF.)

52. Ibid., p. 177 (of Japanese edition).

53. See Tanigawa Michio, "Chūgoku kanryōsei shakai no hitotsu no mikata" 中国官僚制社会の一つの見方 (One view of China's bureaucratic society), *Ajia kuōtarii* アジア・クォータリー 7.1 (January-March 1975), pp. 115–123; included in Tanigawa, *Chūgoku chūsei shakai to kyōdōtai*, pp. 313–324.

54. Karl A. Wittfogel, *Oriental Despotism: A Comparative Study of Total Power*, New Haven and London, Yale University Press, 1963, p. 5. Japanese translation by Ajia keizai kenkyūjo アジア経済研究所, *Tōyōteki sensei shugi* 東洋的専制主義, Ronsōsha, 1961, p. 9.

55. 木田喜代治, *Ajia teki seisan yōshiki no mondai* アジア的生産様式の問題, Iwanami shoten, 1966; and 福富正実, *Ajia teki seisan yōshiki ronsō no fukkatsu: Sekaishi no kihon hōsoku no saikentō* アジア的生産様式論争の復活：世界史の基本法則の再検討, Miraisha, 1969.

56. Moscow, Akademia nauk SSSR, 1964.

57. Jean Chesneaux, "Le mode de production asiatique: quelques perspectives de recherche," *La Pensée* 114 (January-February 1964), pp. 33–55. Japanese translation: "Ajia teki seisan yōshiki: kenkyūjō no jakkan no mitōshi" アジア的生産様式：研究上の若干の見通し, in Honda.

58. Ibid., p. 33.

59. Ferenc Tökei, *Sur le mode de production asiatique*, Budapest, Akadémiai Kiadó, 1966. Japanese translation by Hani Kyōko 羽仁協子, *Ajia teki seisan yōshiki* アジア的生産様式, Miraisha, 1971.

60. Chesneaux, p. 39.

61. Ibid., p. 41.

62. Roger Garaudy, *Le problème chinois*, Paris, Seghers, 1967. Japanese translation by Nohara Shirō 野原四郎, *Gendai Chūgoku to Marukusu shugi* 現代中国とマルクス主義 (Contemporary China and Marxism), Taishūkan shoten, 1970.

63. L.V. Danilova, "Diskussionnye problemy teorii dokapitalisticheskikh obshchestv," in *Problemy dokapitalisticheskikh obshchestv*, Moscow, 1968. Japanese translation in Fukutomi.

64. 酒井角三郎,「封建社会の構造：中国封建制の検討から封建社会への一般理論へ」, *Shisō* 529 (July 1968), pp. 37–54.

65. *Lu-t'ien* 禄田 were lands, in the Ming, given to nobles who had direct control over the land even in the area of rent collection. See Hoshi, p. 423. (JAF)

66. *Chuang-t'ien* 荘田 were lands also given to nobles in the Ming but, unlike the case of *lu-t'ien*, *chuang-t'ien* were administered by an official who collected rents and allocated resources from it. Thus, there was no direct control over the land by the noble. See Hoshi, p. 423. (JAF)

The Medieval Period in China: Society in the Six Dynasties and Sui-T'ang Periods and the "Community"

As we have seen in Part I, the concept of feudalism has not always proven to be an efficacious way of coming to terms with the distinctive historical development of Chinese society. Nonetheless, it is also doubtlessly rash to regard Chinese society as having been sunk from beginning to end in a bureaucratic social stagnation. Perhaps China superseded her antiquity in some distinctive way of her own, as European society succeeded in surmounting the ancient world by entering feudalism. The estimation ventured in Part I was not yet the result of an empirical study. In Part II, I should now like to investigate this prediction in the full concreteness of Chinese history. In the first chapter, I shall consider the reality and logic behind the transcendence of antiquity; and in the second chapter, I shall discuss the image of the medieval period into which this crystallized.

One

Transcending the World of Antiquity

The Principles of Shang and Chou and Their Dissolution

The Importance of the Change of Mandate from Shang to Chou. Did an era in Chinese history properly qualified to be called "ancient" ever exist? If so, what was the nature of the era that replaced it, and by what logic did it do so? Tracing the theme of the transcendence of antiquity in China and how we are to understand it are, to be sure, difficult matters. It is safe to assume that certain severe social dislocations must have accompanied the flow of history in the transcendence of antiquity. Among the great social transformations experienced in China since the inception of historical time were the Shang-Chou transition, the Spring and Autumn–Warring States period, and the late Latter Han–Three Kingdoms era. Theorists have proposed each one as the watershed between ancient and medieval times (i.e., the feudal period). I should like to consider the significance of each of these social upheavals and then pursue these issues from a somewhat different perspective.

The Shang-Chou transition is regarded as the earliest social transformation in Chinese history. The man who first clearly described the significance of this change in mandate from Shang to Chou was Wang Kuo-wei.[1] He argued that whereas the capital cities of the dynastic houses throughout the Shang were located along the lower reaches of the Yellow River in the East, the Chou rose along the upper reaches of the Yellow River in the West and toppled the Shang. This spelled the victory of Western culture over Eastern culture. Thus, in Wang's theory, the Shang-Chou transition was not merely a dynastic change of mandate but a kind of "cultural revolution" as well.

According to Wang Kuo-wei, the content of this "cultural revolution" can be seen in the institutional differences of the Shang and Chou houses. Through the Shang, succession was fraternal, passing between male siblings legitimate and illegitimate alike. In the Chou, father-to-son succession as well as the institution of the inequality of male offspring were established. The latter gave rise to the new institutions of the patriarchal clan (*tsung-fa*)[a] and mourning garb, as well as a system of enfeoffment that determined the functions of sovereign and subject. In addition, not until the Chou dynasty were the temple system and the institution of exogamous marriage established. The basic principles of the Chou institutions, pointed out here by Wang, fixed Chinese ritual for a long time to come thereafter. Thus, Wang saw the origins of Chinese civilization embedded in the Chou and marked off the Shang-Chou as a crucial turning point in China's civilization.

While appraising Wang's theory as a brilliant observation, Naitō Konan argued that the change in the institutions of the Shang and Chou had to be understood as the evolution of eras and not simply as the result of a political incident, the change of dynasties.[2] Naitō regarded the Shang-Chou transition as contiguous and developmental, rather than as a sharp break. He felt that Shang culture was fairly advanced, although this advancement had declined midway. The Chou, who were of different racial stock, inherited a rather developed culture from the Shang.

Kaizuka Shigeki follows Naitō's ideas and has added correctives to Wang Kuo-wei's theory with empirical evidence. Kaizuka points out that although Wang considered the Shang-to-Chou a basic transition from Eastern to Western culture, Shang culture in the later period sought an amalgamation of Eastern and Western cultures. Furthermore, father-to-son inheritance and a feudal system can also already be seen in embryo in the Shang. In short, Kaizuka holds that the Shang-Chou transition was not a sharp rupture but a point of continuity and development.[3]

Other theories have been suggested to explain the Shang-Chou transition, but each of them need not be discussed here.

Although unfamiliar with much of the primary material for this period, I feel that a huge leap in Chinese culture in the period centering around the Shang-Chou changeover is undeniable. The nature of this leap was largely as a takeoff point from a society of primitive clans, as can be seen in the change in inheritance rules cited by Wang Kuo-wei. The Shang house may have tended in this direction but it had not taken the decisive step; thus, the state remained primarily theocratic in character. By contrast, the Chou began regulating its people's lives through ritual systems and laid the firm groundwork for a Chinese culture to be characterized by ethical principles.

The jump from Shang to Chou, from the perspective of social structure, in no way marked the negation of the clan system. Chou rituals were not abstract concepts but real prescriptions for regulating order inside and outside the clan. The clan system did not disintegrate but rather was given order, strengthened, and generalized through ritual systems. We can see how such rules for inheritance, sacrifice, enfeoffment, and marriage were aimed at preserving and strengthening the patriarchal clan. In other words, ritual systems signified the form through which the clan system was civilized. The example of the enfeoffment system demonstrates that blood-relatedness (the principle around which social cohesion existed in clan society) extended to political principles.

Thus, while the Shang-Chou changeover was an event that deserves special mention in China's social history, it did not signify a negation of ancient society. Rather, it is best understood as the actualization of a stride forward from primitive clan society.

The Dissolution of the Principles Underlying Shang and Chou. The second period of change was the Spring and Autumn–Warring States era. After these few centuries of social upheaval, a united empire emerged in the Ch'in-Han period. Politically, the enfeoffment system was transformed into a centralized power, and the aristocratic system (in the sense to be described) into a bureaucracy. Deep social and economic changes, needless to say, lay behind this political transformation. How were the two qualitatively different historical worlds of Shang-Chou and Ch'in-Han linked by this transitional period? What were the continuities and discontinuities between the two eras?

As mentioned, the social principles of Shang and Chou were characterized by blood cohesion in the clan system forming a matching political order. One's position by blood determined one's political position. A particular clan body held political sovereignty. A system of infeudation, already begun in the Shang era, effected the political expansion of familial relations between the king and his relatives. In the Chou system of enfeoffment, this was fully developed, and the system of succession prescribed the bond between the king and the feudal lords and their retainers. Even the relationship between ruling and subordinate clans was no exception. The Shang royal house was tied to different surnamed feudal lords through fictive fraternal bonds; the Chou king's relationship to feudal lords with different surnames was conceptualized as main and branch houses.

The imperial clan and its collateral clans as a whole formed the aristocracy (*shih-tsu*),[b] aside from which were the common people under their control. It appears that these commoners also carried on their own family affairs and as a group offered service to the aristocracy. There is an assortment of arguments surrounding the nature of the bond that brought together the aristocratic group and commoners into a "state" (*kuo*)[c] of the enfeoffed states of the Chou. Kaizuka Shigeki argues that the aristocrats and commoners participated together in the sacrifices to the deities of the earth and grain, but Masubuchi Tatsuo claims that the latter could not take part.[4] Putting aside the correctness of these two theories for now, the substance of the disagreement is reflected in the ordering principle of that time— blood determines politics.

In the Spring and Autumn period, this principle began to be undermined. Characteristic of this era was the development of a rupture between the status order based on blood ties and real power relations, as indicated by the decline in the Chou king's authority and the rapid rise of hegemonic feudal lords. This trend led to a power struggle within the aristocracy until the attempted mediation plans of such men as Tzu-ch'an[d] of Cheng[e] and Kuan-chung[f] of Ch'i,[g] both essentially reconstructions of traditional aristocratic politics. But politics still could not be moved from the principle of blood to that of brute force.

In the time of Confucius, subsequent to that of Kuan-chung and Tzu-ch'an, the task confronted by history was no longer simply the resolution of relations between aristocrats, but it had of necessity become their reaching down to make contact with the nonaristocratic strata. Responding to these new conditions, Confucius sought a reconstruction of the moral order of society. In his famous phrase, he stated: "[There is government] when the prince is prince, and the minister is minister; when the father is father, and the son is son." [5] The proper place for prince and minister, and for father and son, had been taken for granted in the Chou patriarchal clan because they expressed the a priori condition of blood ties in human relations. Now this a priori conditionality was no longer a self-evident norm, however, and herein lies the historical importance of Confucius's words.

Confucius's position under this new reality was not to bury traditional ethics through determination of blood ties but to value it consciously as a morality to be gained through acquired (a posteriori) effort. By the same token, this reveals the polarization of values at the time. The contention between schools in the intellectual world of the Warring States period was a necessary phenomenon caused by the collapse of the principle of clan blood ties. The thoroughly political pragmatism of the Legalists formed the most radical countersupposition to this principle. They rejected all "communitarian" bonds that the people formed on their own, and they demanded that all men be directly under the control of the sovereign as atomized individuals. (See the discussion of Utsunomiya Kiyoyoshi's theory in the next section.) In order to complete this autocracy, a full-fledged bureaucracy was adopted, and officials never possessed any autonomy but were merely the sovereign's servants.

Legalist political views constituted one side of the new type of state in the Spring and Autumn–Warring States period. As the bureaucracy and the centralized system of commanderies and prefectures became more developed, they finally gave birth to the unified Ch'in-Han empire. This might be dubbed the final result of the dissolution of the ancient Shang-Chou state. But what social principle permeated this new historical world? The political principles of the Legalists—to bring the people as atomized individuals under control—doubtlessly constituted one aspect of the Ch'in-Han empire. However, it would be an exaggeration to say that this alone was the sole principle at this stage. The ideas of the Confucians themselves, and in a certain sense this also served as a wellspring for the Legalists, was a view premised on the collapse of the notion of clan blood ties. In actuality, Confucianism eventually gained access to the position of being the Han empire's guiding ideal.

The question of what social principle to apply to an understanding of the Ch'in-Han empire, as touched on in various sections of Part I, became a major topic of postwar East Asian historiography. A wide variety of theories were proposed, starting with the notion of a shift from relations of the clan system to patriarchal slavery. The tendency in recent years has been to focus on the bonds of "community" cohesion of the people who formed the structural foundation for the despotic state.[6] Thus, we have come to adopt a method that does not look at the Ch'in-Han empire solely to see forms of despotism but turns the issue around to look for connections to the world that supported or opposed it. Utsunomiya Kiyoyoshi's work has attempted this effort with the most remarkable methods.[7] I should like now to address this issue, making reference to Utsunomiya's theories.

The Structure of the Ch'in-Han Empire and the Autonomous World

On the Structure of Ch'in-Han Empire. Utsunomiya explained the Ch'in-Han empire as a structure in which the emperor and the people were situated at opposite extremes of the spectrum. The emperor sought to render his power over the people thorough through an individuated, personalized rule, and accordingly his view of the people was the Legalist's atomized notion. The people, however, organized in their daily lives into groups that were united by internal, mutual bonds. The smallest unit was the three-*tsu*[8] family, made up of the three units of the father and mother, wife and children, and siblings. Even when a son grew up and might have his own wife and sons, he lived with his father, mother, and siblings, often as an extended family. Family members managed the farming of their family's land cooperatively.

The father was not necessarily an absolute ruler who controlled the family members and their cooperative life as a
patriarch. Actual family life centered around the young men
and their wives and sons. While the parents received their
respect, they were to be provided for through their childrens'
labor. Thus, the father was the elder of the whole family
group—his connection to the family members carried no stipu-
lation of a ruler-ruled bond. Rather, it was a bond made on the
basis of the ethical awareness of each individual and the central
moral aim of this autonomous ethic—namely, filial piety.

This kinship bond within each autonomous family among
the people was the patrilineage (*tsung-tsu*).[h] There were also
families on the periphery of a patrilineage with distant or no
blood ties, and all of these together made up local village
(*hsiang-tang*)[i] society. A group of elders known as *fu-lao*[j] (or
fu-hsiung)[k] led the patrilineage and local village, whereas general
clan constituents were known as *tzu-ti*.[l] The relationship between *fu-lao* and *tzu-ti* was symbolized as a flesh-and-blood
familial bond of a father and son or an elder and younger
brother; and this bond seems to have operated as an autonomous personal relationship.

If their connection to the emperor was considered heteron-
omous, the people retained the autonomous world of family,
patrilineage, and local village. Also, despite the fact that the
emperor considered the people separate individuals, the "real
life" of the people was built around their mutual "communitarian" solidarity. Thus, the basic principle of the emperor and
that of the people were not merely of a different nature—they
were diametrically opposed. These two underlying principles
were turned into ideologies by the Mohists (and the Legalists)
and the Confucians respectively. The opposing group principles—heteronomy vs. autonomy—which took form in the
Spring and Autumn–Warring States period worked in contradictory and conflicting, as well as cooperative and mutually
penetrating, ways. Together they gave form to the actual social
groupings of the day. Utsunomiya argued that the Ch'in-Han
empire constituted the realization of these historical principles.

One feature of Utsunomiya's theory was his view of the
family. It was Nishijima Sadao (in his earlier theory) and
Masubuchi Tatsuo who had called the family of that time patriarchal, had located in this quality the germinal points of power,

or had tried to argue, respectively, that it was of the same character as and in a supportive relationship to imperial power. Utsunomiya understood the family of that time as a nonpatriarchal, powerless world, and he stressed the qualitatively different principles underlying it and the empire.[9] While this does not avoid the danger of falling into a dualism, Utsunomiya's historical conception of the Ch'in-Han empire established an entirely new perspective. Although he assumed that, in the process of the dissolution of cohesion based on clan blood ties of the Shang-Chou era, society dispersed into three-*tsu* families, Utsunomiya's view led to an interpretation that the society under the Ch'in-Han family system had in fact inherited the autonomous quality of clan society from the Shang and Chou.[10] Thus, it appears that Confucianism acted as its carrier in ideological form.

Nonetheless, in certain respects, Shang-Chou and Ch'in-Han were qualitatively different. As noted earlier, the founding principle of Shang and Chou politics and society was the one-to-one mapping into the political realm of the order of blood ties. The blood unit was the political unit; relations (or their imitation) within the clan were nothing short of political relationships. However, under the system of three-*tsu* families, the result of the dispersal of the ancient clans, a political world could not take shape on its own. Rather, the political world could emerge only after having transcended individual families. An autonomous world of the family could not (without undergoing change) give form to a political world. The world was polarized into the autonomous realm and the political realm. The bipolar construction of the emperor and the people in Utsunomiya's theory was clearly the result of a functional differentiation of society in the earlier period.

On what basis did these two differentiated realms mutually interact to form the united world of the Ch'in-Han empire? It appears that Utsunomiya could not avoid a dualism here because this basis was not clearly indicated. I shall offer next a simple attempt at investigating this problem.

The Autonomous World and the Political World. The spatial expanse of what Utsunomiya called the "autonomous world" was the area in which families came into contact through their daily lives—the hamlet or *li*.[11] The hamlet was the configuration of the residences of families, with a standard size of one hundred households, but a diverse number in actuality. It was surrounded by a mud wall, and intercourse with the outside was carried on through the hamlet gate. Residents of the hamlet attended to many matters cooperatively, such as harvest rites, public works, and defense. The hamlet formed a territorial "community." If a number of hamlets came together, they formed fortified towns known as *hsiang*[m] and *t'ing*.[n] A number of these would coalesce into a prefecture or *hsien*.[o] Thus, the ranking in the system of commanderies (*chün*)[p] and prefectures was *hsiang-t'ing-li*, though it was not a simple subordinating structure.

The *li* or hamlet was an autonomous unit led by a group of elders, and from the elders in each village a Thrice Venerable for the *hsiang*[q] was selected to manage local education. From the *hsiang* Thrice Venerables was chosen a prefectural Thrice Venerable[r] who was equivalent in rank to the local official beneath the prefect. In short, an autonomous structure with the hamlet as its basic unit extended from the hamlet through the *hsiang* to the prefectural level. This indicates the spatial scope of the daily contacts between families by virtue of patrilineal and local village relationships. However, the prefecture, or more likely the *hsiang*, was the outside limit of the autonomous world. (Commandery Thrice Venerables[s] and kingdom Thrice Venerables[t] were also installed on occasion, but they seem to have been mere figureheads.) Over on the other side of this boundary were the prefecture, commandery, and the center—the political world.

The issue at hand is how the autonomous world and the political world were connected. At the time of the Ch'en Sheng[u] Rebellion at the end of the Ch'in, the elders of P'ei prefecture murdered the prefect, who had tenaciously held out for the Ch'in, and tried to install Liu Pang[v] in his place. Liu Pang turned them down, saying: "I fear that my abilities are superficial and that I am unable to fulfill my duties to protect my brethren. . . . I pray that you select a capable man."[12] He subsequently was selected Prefect of P'ei and began the project of unifying the realm.

Judging from the details of this case, the *raison d'être* of the prefect for the local elders and clan members lay in his capacity to protect their lives and bring them peace of mind in their livelihood. Aware of the consciousness of his fellow locals, Liu Pang induced them to murder the Ch'in prefect so that he could take over the position. Two years later he entered the Ch'in capital at Hsien-yang and called together the elders and notables of the prefectures in order to make his famous declaration of the Three Articles of Law. He said to them: "The reason that I have come is entirely to eliminate evil on behalf of the elders. There is no room for tyranny [like the Ch'in dynasty's]. Have no fear."[13] These words set forth directly that Liu Pang's personal mission was to wipe out the onerous laws of the Ch'in and bring peace to the lives of the people.

The late Moriya Mitsuo used these examples to argue in the following way. Liu Pang's strength originally derived from his group of vagabonds and chivalrous men who had drifted away from their localities, but this limited the extent of his might. He qualified as sovereign of a new dynasty by receiving the support of the local elders and by using their capacity to lead. In this way, Liu Pang was able, according to Moriya, to jump from the position of being merely the chief of a band of chivalrous spirits to that of autocratic monarch. Thus, he argues that state power in its germinal form rested in such groups of gallant men, but these groups required the support of local society to transform themselves into a state.[14]

If we push this argument one step further, whether or not state power (or a band of gallant men as its embryonic form) was supported by local society depended on the extent to which it acted as protector of local society. Local society and state power formed a kind of support-protection bond. *In this sense*, it is not necessarily unreasonable to understand the rationale for the state to lie in its functions of preserving and sustaining local society.

Providing these two functions in local society had historical limitations that prevented them from being fully carried out by local society itself. It was unavoidable that mechanisms to do so were beyond the means of local society. The state—a band of gallant hearts in its rudimentary form and a military-bureaucratic apparatus in its completed form—played this role. This role for the state bestowed a certain superiority on itself and emerged as despotic control over local society. In its most extreme form, this constituted Legalistic control. In the Ch'in era, even for people to meet and chat was punishable as a capital offense, and this was an extreme denial of the autonomous cohesion of the people. Liu Pang's Three Articles of Law promised to eliminate such severity in government. The Ch'in fell and was replaced by the Han, which guaranteed the autonomous life of the people.

As we have seen thus far, the Ch'in-Han empire in one respect clearly carried on Shang-Chou society. In Shang-Chou society, the political world and the autonomous world were integrated in an undifferentiated whole, and when it dissolved, these two worlds split apart. The mission of the Ch'in-Han empire was to reconstitute the bond in a new form. While the autonomous world inherited the three-*tsu* family as its basic unit, it lacked political independence in and of itself. This limitation gave birth at one pole to the political world in the form of empire. Thus, at the same time that these two worlds opposed each other, they also seemed to complement each other. One senses that with the passage of time the basic trend of the Ch'in-Han empire was toward the harmonious reintegration of the two worlds through mutual intervention and mutual penetration. I should like to address this phenomenon from the perspective of the bureaucracy.

One feature that distinguishes the Ch'in-Han period from the Shang-Chou era is the development of bureaucracy in the Ch'in-Han. If we can generalize ruling status in the Chou dynasty to be composed of people known as *shih*,ᵂ then the *shih* was a status given to those born into the ruling clans and carried with it particular religious and military functions. The upheavals of the Spring and Autumn and Warring States periods broke down this status system, and a bureaucratic body was formed in its place. Who made up this new ruling stratum of "bureaucrats"?

Confucius spoke of the human qualities befitting the new rulers of the new age, and he called the men who possessed such qualities *shih*. By putting it this way, he may have implied the vapidity of the old *shih* system supported by principles of blood relations. Confucius tried to compensate for this emptiness by painting an ideal of a new *shih* based on personal qualities. In actuality, the *shih* had to be practitioners of family morality, and this practice itself took place in government. Thus, here was the ideal of an immanent consistency between morality and politics; and the original model of Confucius's conception was the *shih* of the Chou dynasty, the ritual—and hence political—system. Confucius called for this with a method not bound by the status system: old wine poured into new leather skins.

An interesting problem would be to see how other thinkers of the Spring and Autumn–Warring States period conceived of the *shih*, but we cannot go into that here. Under the Ch'in unification, political utilitarianism according to Legalist principles constituted the ideal for bureaucracy. Thus, the baseline was the extent to which an official contributed to the monarch, and the inner personal qualities of the official himself were irrelevant. On this point, there was no fundamental change in the Han. The political ideal in the first half of the Former Han could not erase Legalist principles in this one respect, and this was one reason people felt the autocratic nature of the Han empire. In the recruitment of bureaucrats at the time, when a meritorious official had no son to whom to bequeath his appointment, weight was placed for selection on Legalist officials knowledgeable in the law and practical administrative work. This indicates well the nature of the bureaucracy at that time.

The transformation from a bureaucratic system of this sort is complicated by the period when Emperor Wu[x] ruled in the Former Han (140–87 B.C.). He instituted a system of local recommendation and election (*hsiang-chü li-hsüan*),[y] and the man who proposed the idea was Tung Chung-shu.[z] The Emperor's plan called for the eradication of the abuses of the earlier hereditary bureaucratic system by enabling each commandery to recommend annually wise men to be high-level expectant officials. The immediate consequences of this policy are unclear, but eventually a system of recommendation of Men of Filial Piety and Incorruptibility (*hsiao-lien*)[aa] began and by the Latter Han it had been institutionalized.

The significance of this local recommendation and election system lay in the fact that through it the government appointed men of talent based on popular opinion. It was, in effect, a form of bureaucratic recruitment through cooperation between officials and the populace. The criteria for appointment were filiality and integrity—living a moral life in local society—not simply administrative capacity. This form of appointment served the function of absorbing not just the appointee but local society itself within the purview of state power.

Intertwined as this was with the adoption of Confucianism, proposed by Tung Chung-shu, it produced the conditions for the political world and the autonomous world to be reunited under the superior position of the former. This was not an immanent unification of the two on the basis of a status system based on blood ties. Reconsolidation could only occur, once that sort of unity had been ruptured, under the condition of the destruction of such a status system. Thus, the people who bore the task of this reunification were the Confucian literati of the Han dynasty. Was not then the universe of the Chou consummated within an even greater cycle?

The End of Empire and the Transcendence of the Foundations of Antiquity

The Theoretical Consequences of the Perfection of Empire. If we consider the Han empire the perfection of the ancient state, then within this image of perfection we need to find the moment at which historical development reached an impasse and growth switched to decline. A period of severe social dislocation in no way inferior to that of the Spring and Autumn–Warring States period occurred, to be sure, at the time of the collapse of the Han. Let us take a closer look at the import of these disorders from the perspective just outlined.

If we accept the proposal in its most superficial aspect that the Han empire was the perfection of the ancient state, then this is borne out by the very extent of Han territory. In Naitō Konan's periodization, antiquity is divided in two: the earlier period of the formation of Chinese culture and the later period when, with the spread of Chinese culture outward, Chinese history was transformed into East Asian history.[15] Generally speaking, these two periods can be understood as before and after the establishment of the Ch'in-Han empire. The characteristic of the later period, according to Naitō, whereby China's cultural development beyond her borders transformed Chinese history into the history of East Asia, implied that the development of Chinese culture was not limited to that of a single state but unfolded to give structure to a world history that included all the ethnic groups living on China's peripheries. From this perspective, calling the Ch'in-Han empire the perfection of the ancient state implies that it reached its pinnacle as a world empire.

To be somewhat more specific, the project of attempting to attain perfection as a world empire had already begun under Ch'in Shih-huang-ti.[ab] His military exploits attest to this effect: he drove the Hsiung-nu off to the North, finished the Great Wall, attacked Nan-yüeh,[ac] and attempted to extend a system of commanderies and prefectures in the northern part of Vietnam. However, it was not until after the reign of the Emperor Wu that one sees this project firmly entrenched. From this time, a reversal in power relations between the Han and the Hsiung-nu brought the lands of Tibet, Korea, and Nan-yüeh under the direct dominion of the Han dynasty, and Han culture spread to the west of Central Asia and as far eastward as Japan. As Naitō put it, the development of Chinese culture externally led to the formation of a world of "East Asian history."

Nonetheless, the birth of this world empire spawned a new problem for itself. This was not the result of an ephemeral situation, such as the secession through rebellion of the lands of alien peoples which had once been occupied by China, as had occurred at the end of the Ch'in. Rather, this would be a qualitatively new problem of holding onto territory gained by the Han through the successful conquest of China's border regions. The Hsiung-nu, who began to subside from the reign of Emperor Wu on, split into Northern and Southern halves in the Latter Han, and the Southern Hsiung-nu migrated back to their homeland. The inner reason for these developments can be found in the integral elements of a shift in the power relations between Han and Hsiung-nu, as well as the penetration of Han culture into Hsiung-nu society. The political and cultural superiority of the Han caused Hsiung-nu society to be subsumed under the Han empire and finally brought on its self-destruction.

The two tribes Ti[ad] and Ch'iang,[ae] which had come into closer contact with the Han as the Hsiung-nu weakened, were both largely forced to move to territory within the empire. The racial conflict this stirred up led to frequent troubles. The great

Ch'iang rebellion at the beginning of the second century A.D. severely impoverished the Han dynasty. This provides a fine illustration of the reverberatory results of the success of Han external expansion. Naitō's first period, "antiquity," eventually brings about, together with its perfection, its own demise.

According to Naitō, the period from the second half of the Latter Han through the Western Chin composes a transitional era between "antiquity" (period one) and the "medieval era" (period two). Thus, this "medieval era"—namely, from the Six Dynasties through the middle of the T'ang—was a period in which the alien races came to a self-awareness and extended their influence back into the Chinese interior. Naitō's method tries to understand the historical development of Chinese society as two vectors: the external expansion of Chinese culture and the internal penetration of the border races awakened by Chinese expansion. Thus, the Han empire reached the peak of its external expansion, and then its demise supplied the turning point for the reverse tide it had itself unleashed.

Since I have analyzed elsewhere the problem of conflict resulting from the Han expansion,[16] I shall withhold further comment. Here I should like to consider the issue of the internal expansion of Han culture. Was there not similar historical logic at work in the permeation of the power of the Han empire down to the ground level of Chinese society and in Han external expansion? In other words, the closer the ancient world came to completion through the Han empire's deep thrusts into society, the more it seems a qualitatively different world was emerging therein. If this prediction proves true, then I believe we can find here both the logic and the actuality for the transcendence of the ancient world.

As we have seen, in the process of the completion of the Han empire, the political world incorporated within itself the autonomous world. Although it was a consolidation of two worlds through the hegemony of the former, did not the autonomous world entertain the possibility of striving for its own completion so that it could achieve its own hegemony? The earliest manifestation of this development in the Latter Han was a literati movement in the factional strife of the two streams (to be discussed).

The problem of land annexation, which had already surfaced during the reign of Emperor Wu—something that Tung Chung-shu pointed out—was worked out at the end of the Former Han in the policies of Shih Tan[af] and K'ung Kuang[ag] for limitations on the amount of land and number of servants one could have. The fact that it was obstructed by maternal relatives and court favorites from being implemented, however, presaged the political situation in the subsequent Latter Han. From the middle of the Latter Han, maternal relatives and eunuchs echoed this strife, monopolized political power, and rapidly deepened their personal hold on state power. This progressed in a close relationship to the issue of land annexation. After the debacle of the Wang Mang[ah] reforms, which carried Shih Tan's aims one drastic step further, the attempt to restrain with political power the annexation of land and people was no longer undertaken. Or rather, political power itself became engulfed in a wave of rapidly advancing large landholdings and class differentiation.

In particular, after Emperor Huan[ai] relied on the might of eunuchs to exterminate the maternal relatives of the Liang[aj] family in the middle of the second century A.D., the shadow of "eunuch despotism" was cast over the imperial government. Their baneful influence spread widely through society. Not only did they directly oppress people and frantically try to increase their private property but also, because of their interdependence with the local great clans and their mutual plans for private gain, they were able to extend their influence to every corner of society. They brought about a privatization of power throughout the entire state structure. In this way, the dissolution of the state reached the point where it could no longer be staved off during the reigns of Emperor Huan (r. 147–167) and Emperor Ling[ak] (r. 168–188) at the end of the Latter Han.

In the middle of the Former Han, Tung Chung-shu indicted the annexation of land and proposed that limitations be set on large landholdings, but what Tung was criticizing was not simply the confiscation of the people's land. He was pointing out that the state in its entirety at that time was being transformed into a mechanism for the exploitation and oppression of the people, and he was criticizing this by analogy with society under the well-field system of high antiquity. His idea of turning the Han dynasty into an ideal Confucian state was far from realistic. The people could never expect such a moral life under these political, social, and economic circumstances. Thus, Tung Chung-shu's plan for limiting the size of landholdings can be regarded as an initiative premised on the structure of a moral Confucian world that looked upon antiquity as ideal.

More than two centuries after Tung Chung-shu's time, it would be Pure Stream (*Ch'ing-liu*)[17] literati who moved to resist the political and economic state of affairs which had all but become desperate by the end of the Latter Han. Where in the world did these Pure Stream literati come from historically?

The Universality of the Pure Stream Movement. This issue was examined comprehensively a number of years ago by Kawakatsu Yoshio.[18] Kawakatsu criticized Yang Lien-sheng[al] who had argued that the opposition between the Pure Stream and the Turbid Stream (*Chou-liu*),[am] in the final analysis, was discord between two groups of great clans—eunuch great clans and bureaucratic great clans—over the acquisition of political power. Kawakatsu argued that the base of support of the Pure Stream literati lay not in the great clans themselves but in a *public opinion* that transcended both clan organization and regionalism and supported them without regard to status or class. In other words, members and nonmembers of great clans, with a single ideological platform, formed one large sphere of influence that united a widespread public opinion.

The platform, this public opinion, was a concept of the state which professed its legitimacy against the existing perversion of the state; it embodied a Confucian conception of the state. The fact that maternal relatives and eunuchs held sovereign power constituted a perversion of what the Han state should have been; similarly, the fact that high-minded literati were excluded while wicked rascals swarmed about the reins of power was inexcusable in their minds. Kawakatsu argued, thus, that the Pure Stream literati sought a solidarity of three groups—the emperor, the literati, and the people—from the shared position of a conception of a fair and just state. As this conception expanded in the form of a nationwide public opinion, it exerted considerable pressure on the central government.

Within the Pure Stream sphere, character evaluations (such

as the "first day of the month criticism")[19] based on a notion of what a literatus should be according to Confucian value standards were exchanged. These evaluations severely repudiated the corrupt government's bureaucratic recruitment practices, and the literati as the voice of public opinion formed a unified circle. They forged mutual bonds of teachers and friends as well as a kind of master-servant bond known as *men-sheng ku-li*[an] (retainers) to men of renown. The associations thus formed maintained their mutual contacts and received support from the overall literati body.

With the expansion and strengthening of the Pure Stream force, the Latter Han state lost its substance and finally brought on an era of warlordism. Kawakatsu argued that the literati who carried on the spirit of the Pure Stream group preserved their shared feelings and retained their mutual contacts even under warlord rule. This indicated their supranational, universal position, which transcended the individual militarist states. The Six Dynasties aristocracy, which existed as the ruling class in society on a plane above changes in dynastic houses, were the successors of these literati.

The preceding was an outline of Kawakatsu's theory. The basic motif was his placing of the origin of the Six Dynasties aristocracy in the Pure Stream literati. His theory was unique in that he interpreted the Six Dynasties aristocracy as distinct from the great clans and as transcendent over them. The great clans were groupings in which kinsmen in a locality were united around a main family and in which additionally were included non-blood-related dependents such as "guests" and bodyguards. They possessed huge tracts of land and held sway over the local countryside. The great clans, however, were not necessarily aristocrats. Aristocrats owed their honored position to status, not simply to the possession of power. Here, Kawakatsu argued, was the kind of universality enjoyed by the aristocratic class.

In short, Kawakatsu understood the resistance movement of the Pure Stream literati as a movement of intellectuals rising above the Han empire, which had become corrupt and had deviated from its basic nature; and he linked the movement to the subsequent Six Dynasties aristocracy. Thus far in conformity with the points of this chapter, his argument describes one side of the fierce conflict in which the autonomous world, being incorporated into the political world of the Han empire through the local recommendation system, was gradually maturing toward a transcendence of the empire which it had supported ideally. Nonetheless, could something that tried to bolster the empire conceptually really transcend it? The historical facts reveal that their movement was dealt crushing blows in two separate suppressions known as the proscriptions against scholarly cliques (*tang-ku*).[ao] The "first shock" leading to the destruction of the Han empire was administered by a different sort of movement, the Yellow Turban rebellion. We are left with a vague sense of uneasiness as to whether or not the Pure Stream movement did in fact transcend the Han empire. Masubuchi Tatsuo's critique of Kawakatsu's argument was much concerned with this problem.[20]

Critique of the Pure Stream Movement. Masubuchi's argument goes as follows. Kawakatsu tended to conceptualize the actual activities of the intellectual class of the day. Their activities were in no sense uniform, for in addition to those men who supported the Pure Stream officials, there was also a group of intellectuals who, although they had received the same Confucian training, adopted a different mode of action. They were in fact critical of the Pure Stream movement. For "famous scholars" (*ming-shih*)[ap] to meet with repression was actually considered an honor; this was the ethos by which Pure Stream literati honored moral integrity.

Yet, as can be seen in the cases of Shen-t'u P'an[aq] and Yüan Hung,[ar] there were people who foresaw the factional intrigues and saved their lives by escaping. Masubuchi argues that they were all men with reputations for goodness in their local villages, but they did not respond to the call of the Pure Stream bureaucrats and held firm to an eremitic attitude of a whole life of nonservice. While they were indeed critical of the eunuchs, they also voiced an exceedingly harsh position toward the pompous political arguments of Pure Stream adherents, the so-called *fu-hua chiao-hui*[as] (superficial intercourse). Why was this the case?

Masubuchi continues that even though the Pure Stream movement grew through its advocacy of true purity and upright-

ness, in actual fact it contained elements of impure motives—
"guys looking for fame and seeking profit," as Hu San-hsing[at]
(1230–1287; a commentator on the *Tzu-chih t'ung-chien*)[21] de-
rided them. The capital (then at Lo-yang) was a place where
heroes and chivalrous spirits assembled, and the Imperial College (T'ai-hsüeh)[au] there with over 30,000 students was a scene
of burning political debate. The residences of the "famous
scholars" were always packed with guests, and as the expression that emerged from this—"scaling the Dragon Gate" (*teng
Lung-men*)[av]—suggests, people sought an opportunity for
government service through friendships with these "famous
scholars." And there clearly were a goodly number of such
people thirsty for publicity.

It was said that Tou Wu,[aw] a man of outer court origins who
was praised by Imperial College students as "the trustworthy
Tou Yu-p'ing[ax] [Wu] of the realm," distributed presents to the
students from the Emperor and Empress. Yet, did he not make
skillful use of public opinion among the students, who were
highly critical of the eunuchs, and did he not try to strengthen his
own political position in opposition to the eunuchs? This being
the case, did Tou Wu and the students not contradict themselves by attacking the eunuchs as a corrupt force while falling
into the same status by arrogating political power to themselves?
Perhaps this is the reason why the eremitic scholars refused to
go along with the Pure Stream movement.

Hu San-hsing's criticism of the Pure Stream movement
comes to us primarily from ideas expressed in Ch'en Yüan's[ay]
work, *T'ung-chien Hu-chu piao-wei*[az] (An elucidation of Hu
[San-hsing]'s commentary on the *Tzu-chih t'ung-chien*). Ch'en
felt Hu's criticism was a satire directed at the malodorous
adhesion between the prime minister and the Imperial College
students of the late Southern Sung, the case at hand for Hu.
Following Ch'en's idea, Masubuchi suggested carrying this
argument further to reinvestigate earlier conceptions of the
Pure Stream movement.

As we have noted, Kawakatsu sought to explain the historical development from the Latter Han into the Six Dynasties
period in sequential fashion by locating the origins of the Six
Dynasties aristocracy in the Pure Stream literati of the late
Latter Han. He saw them as having transcended the Han dy-

nasty, but Masubuchi's criticism pointed to the limitations of the Pure Stream literati and stressed the fact that their political clout would not necessarily overcome the decadence of the Latter Han state—it actually possessed a similar aspect in itself. Masubuchi must be highly praised for offering subsequent scholarship a new perspective in educing the existence of a critical, eremetic intelligentsia who did not follow the path taken by the Pure Stream movement.

Shortly thereafter, Kawakatsu responded to Masubuchi's critique and added to the complexity of the issue.[22] While accepting Masubuchi's criticism, Kawakatsu offered the following rebuttal. The resistance movement against control of the empire by eunuch power was an immense effort covering a period of fifty years from the latter half of the second century into the beginning of the third. It began with the political criticism of the Pure Stream literati, gave birth here to what Masubuchi called eremitic scholars, and later exploded in a revolutionary mass movement of poor peasants—the Yellow Turbans. From this macroscopic perspective, it is impossible to view the eremites as cut off from the Pure Stream sphere of influence. Also, the facts themselves indicate that the two were closely linked. Kawakatsu argues that there were men with eremitic proclivities among the Pure Stream literati and cases of close friendship between these two sorts of men.

What then was the social basis for a resistance movement of intellectuals such as the Pure Stream group and the hermit clique? To answer this question, Kawakatsu points to the fact that local society at the time had lost its original "communitarian" order and that it had been transformed into an arena of conflict among great clans. Certain segments of these great clans were linked to eunuch power and tried to destroy their rivals with eunuch backing. Thus was formed the "Real Power" alignment between eunuchs and great clans.

Great clan members estranged from this alliance and intellectuals who looked angrily upon the long-standing domination of local areas by the great clans offered resistance activities in a variety of forms. One of these was the Pure Stream movement, and another was the orientation toward the life of a hermit who, despairing that there was no recourse for the situation, sought to reject any contact with contemporary politics. Both cases were products of a dilemma that stretched across an internal contradiction within the great clans: a struggle between the aspirations of the great clans to expand themselves and a spirit of self-restraint based on Confucian training. This might be restated as a conflict between the destructive and preservative elements of the great clans with regard to the local village. If we look back at the theory presented by Kawakatsu in his earlier essay—namely, the notion of an aristocracy as a universal class transcending individual great clans—we can trace how this theme develops and how this internal contradiction inherent in the great clans was transcended in the actual movement.

One part of the Pure Stream literati which possessed this inner contradiction lost its resistance power because of the repressive proscription on cliques, while the mantle of resistance remained principally on the shoulders of the eremitic men of letters and the people. The intellectuals who resisted looked for a means of survival at this time which was now shifting from the resistance of the Pure Stream to that of the eremites. The hermit types had earned the esteem of the people as sages and concentrated on forming a new moral "community" with themselves in charge. Kawakatsu makes use of an essay by R. A. Stein, "Remarques sur les mouvements du taoïsme politico-religieux au IIe-siècle ap. J-C,"[23] to speak of a new world structured in this way, which was in fact something sought after by the popular religious revolutionary movement of the Yellow Turbans. Hermit intellectuals and the populace, the two elements of this resistance movement, he argues, built a new universe with this bond they forged.

While Masubuchi distinguished the Pure Stream literati and eremitic scholars by their different points of view, Kawakatsu tries to see their connections and their dynamic interplay in the broad sweep of history. Nonetheless, we still do not have an exhaustive, logical treatment of these two types of intellectual stance raised by Masubuchi. Once we have pinpointed this problem, I believe it can offer us a glimpse of how the political principles supporting the Han empire were overcome by these men. I should now like to offer my own impressions of this period.

The Populace and a Shift in Ideas among the Intelligentsia during the Han. Kawakatsu's macroscopic overview and the problems specific to the Pure Stream literati raised by Masubuchi seem to argue opposing positions, but in fact there is a point at which we can understand them in a unified manner. When we compare the stances of Pure Stream literati and the eremitic men of letters, we can see that the former were attacking the eunuchs from a conception of order that had existed in the past, while the latter were critical of such a relativistic approach itself and tried to plant themselves at a point from which to transcend that conception of order. This entailed a fundamental shift from the established position of Han intellectuals represented by the Pure Stream literati. If the Pure Stream faction is seen as no better than the Turbid Stream, then the importance of this *shift* among the intellectuals will be reduced. In actuality, the Pure Stream literati at least did not give sanction to the pursuit of self-interest as would befit the Turbid Stream, for this was the essence of their position as literati. Hence, the problem is twofold: Why, as Masubuchi notes, does their movement evoke a certain sense of opacity? And, why does a movement that stands for justice somehow link up with individual personal profit?

This contradictory construction of arguing that moral integrity gives rise to personal profit seems to have been based on the Han political notion that moral values are directly tied to political values. Morality and learning cohered uniformly with political authority and thus formed a completed imperial structure through the Former Han program of solely honoring Confucian scholars, particularly through the local recommendation system. Morality and learning, which would originally have found their sustenance in a critique of this system, diluted their own essences and adhered to the system.

The attack on eunuchs by the Pure Stream faction was a resistance from within the system, and thus the means used in attacking political opponents was their authority as officials of the empire. The fact that Imperial College students and Pure Stream officials praised some maternal relatives, as in the case of Tou Wu, was an inevitable result that their position bred. Also, the fact that they were often criticized in word and deed as "superficial" (*fu-hua*)[ba] and "hypocritical" (*wei-shan*)[bb] was not unrelated to the institutionalization of morality. Masubuchi notes the phenomenon of a morality lacking in substance among the literati of the time, which he calls a "nominalization and externalization of the standards of value," but we have to see at the root of this phenomenon the institutionalization and vulgarization of morality and learning.

It was an expression of the Han empire complete. Political authority, grounded in morality and learning, towered above as something righteous and wonderful. At its social base was the autonomous world formed around the lives of individual families. And the Confucian moral practitioners who represented this world were absorbed into the power of the empire through the system of local recommendation.

As Kawakatsu argues, the Pure Stream literati derived their authority from a conception of order in the empire legitimized in this way. Yet, however justified it was, it guaranteed their status as appointed officials of the state. Also, the adherence of local society to political power brought about an inevitable dissolution of the world as they had known it. Thus, when the conception of order in the empire lost its substance, the sense of justice in the minds of the Pure Stream literati became even more righteous. The more they emphasized only moralisms, the greater grew the danger that they lacked a foothold in reality.

The people who discerned this emptiness in both the words and deeds of the Pure Stream faction were the members of the eremitic group. These hermits were groping to lead their lives in such a way as to transcend the empire and its conception of order upon which the Pure Stream people based their existences. For the Pure Stream literati, the Han empire was a permanent, indestructible universe, the kingdom on earth to realize Confucian morality. It was the universe in which notions of morality and learning were to be embodied by politics. Thus, they could not cast doubt upon the sanctity of "politics," and it was they who became the legitimate bearers of politics. In the Chou era, the *shih* had borne the responsibility that politics correspond to the ritual system, and it was a structure essentially no different from this that dominated the consciousness of the Pure Stream literati. Once this confidence was broken, the Han empire would be on the verge of demise.

What directly annulled the perpetuity and sanctity of the Han was, of course, the Yellow Turban uprising. According to Kawakatsu, this rebellion was a movement in search of a new "communitarian" world. However, it was not only the Yellow Turbans who repudiated the perpetuity and sanctity of the Han universe. The eremitic men of learning, avant-garde intellectuals of their day, cleared away the intellectual dimension of conquering the Han by abandoning their place in the establishment. Kawakatsu argues that a bond of spiritual solidarity formed between these intellectuals and the common people and seems to have given shape to the basic structure of social groups of the time, as seen first in the Yellow Turbans. This new solidarity forged between the intellectuals and the people did not give rise solely to a political movement to overthrow the dynasty. Apparently, it suggested as well the starting point for a new age that would transcend the formative principles themselves of China's ancient world that had been ceaselessly maturing since the Shang and Chou. I should like to address this issue in the next chapter.

Two

The Medieval "Community" and Aristocratic Society

The "Communitarian" Structure of Groups in the Wei-Chin Period

The "Communitarian" Orientation of Early Taoism. As we saw in the previous chapter, the kinship order of Shang-Chou society provided a mapping for the political order. In other words, the intrinsic unity of morality and politics functioned as its basic principle. The subsequent society of the Ch'in and Han eras basically lay within the framework of this principle, or rather a reorganization and expansion of it. As time proceeded, however, this social principle eventually became devitalized.

The dissolution of the local village system, one form of "community" in the ancient period, accompanied the phenomenon of the privatization of privilege under a variety of facades: the privatization of state power by maternal relatives and eunuchs, the development of huge landholdings, and the emergence and increase in the number of subordinated people. In the cultural arena, ceremonies to the "god of the soil" (*she*)[bc]—a form of "communitarian" religious faith in the villages—were transformed into individual faith and gave rise to many kinds of popular beliefs concerned more with individual well-being. In short, the decline of a public-oriented principle that had penetrated every aspect of earlier society proved irreversible.

People did not, however, fail to resist this dissolution. The eremitic scholars from the intelligentsia refused to commit themselves to the political world, and Taoists, including many among the populace, took as their personal precepts the restraint of self-interest and a devotion to work for the public. The Taoists would not affirm the trend toward privatization of rights in society but rather aimed at a new bond of solidarity between people on the basis of a rejection and surmounting of this trend. This cohesive bond between people was no longer a natural one of kinship, as in the past, but one of a decidedly ethical, religious nature. The restraint of self-interest provided the crucial moment for the cohesion of this "communitarian" world being sought again.

Let us look at the example of the Five Pecks of Rice religious group, which built a state based on the unity of religion and politics in Szechwan during the Three Kingdoms period. The members of this group built public lodgings known as "charitable inns" (*i-she*),[bd] stocked rice and meat donated by believers, and prepared for the convenience of visitors. If a visitor took a portion larger than personally necessary, they felt he would receive retribution and be stricken with illness.[24] "Visitors" here implied people who, having left their native village for reasons of famine or war, led a life roaming about other regions. The followers of the religion divided their own life resources for such strangers, and those wayfarers and unfamiliar faces who received their help made it a rule that they would not take more than was necessary. In this way, a personal act of self-restraint on both sides formed a solidarity within the religious group. It was a solidarity that went one step beyond bonds of kinship in that it was mediated by an ethical consciousness.

This phenomenon was not limited to the Five Pecks of Rice group. The *Pao-p'u-tzu* of Ko Hung[25] introduced the various "moral injunctions of the way"[26] as follows:

> Those who seek long life ... rejoice in others' good fortune, sympathize with others' hardship, assist others in emergencies, and come to the aid of the impoverished, bring harm to no living creature, do not openly exhort calamities upon others; where you are successful, be happy in others' success, and where you fail, be unhappy if others fail; be not haughty, nor boastful, nor jealous, nor flattering, nor secretive in the wish to harm others.

This clearly shows that the essential spirit of these Taoist groups was a transcendence of self in practice. The followers sought "long life" (immortality) by observing their religious precepts, a world of the highest good for the individual attained by self-transcendence. While this overcame the kinship world of antiquity, it simultaneously spelled a transcendence over that which destroyed that world. One might venture so far as to say that we have here the logical structure for the sublation of the "communitarian" world itself through a transcendence of that which destroyed the ancient "communitarian" world.

When we look at the trends of intellectuals and the people at the end of the Latter Han, we sense an orientation toward a "communitarian" universe of a higher order, as we saw earlier.[27] But how did this inclination take root in the subsequent social structure?

Rebellion and the Formation of Medieval Centers of Population. The decisive moment for the breakup of the Han empire was the Yellow Turban rebellion. Unity of political power completely dissolved, and the political situation rushed forward into the confusion of the Three Kingdoms period. The Chin was to gain control over a reunified political authority, but success was momentary as the independence of the alien peoples threw North China into severe political disorder once again. Until the latter half of the fourth century, when the Northern Wei brought stability to North China, the northern region was in a state of upheaval for about two hundred years. How did these various intellectual currents intent on overcoming the basic principles of antiquity, as seen in the late Latter Han, survive amidst political chaos over two centuries?

It would be rash to consider these currents buried and extinguished in the high seas of politics, because in this era of hardship people had to go on living. The thoroughly enervated central government could no longer ensure the continued existence of the people, and the people accordingly had to plan for it themselves, all the while avoiding the fighting of the militarists. But, since they could not live in isolation, they formed groups of various natures and devised methods for survival. These groups themselves gave expression to a modus vivendi under dire circumstances. They formed the social groundwork that enabled people to deal with the blinding changes wrought by events in the political sphere. The logic of history, as reconstructed earlier, seems to merge with these groups, and I should like now to base these observations in some concrete examples.

Recent scholars have noted the great changes that transpired in the history of Chinese population centers from the Latter Han through the Wei-Chin period. One of these changes was the emergence of the *ts'un*.[be] According to the regulations on households in the K'ai-yuan era (713–741) of the T'ang dynasty, there was no difference between a city and a rural town in the T'ang, as all population sites were united by a "village" system: an urban "village" was called a *fang*[bf] while a rural "village" was called a *ts'un*.

Miyakawa Hisayuki's essay, "Rikuchō jidai no son ni tsuite" (On the *ts'un* of the Six Dynasties period),[28] offers a historical explanation for this. In the Han dynasty, the center of population in town and country alike was generally the hamlet (*li*). Later, Miyakawa points out, there developed a distinction between urban and rural areas which, by the T'ang dynasty, had become institutionalized, as described earlier. He notes that only from the Three Kingdoms period on did the word *ts'un* become a new expression for rural population areas, as a result of this differentiation. The disruption to the Han local village system made people, who had moved to avoid the warfare, form new living areas for self-protection. The sites picked for these areas were not uniform and were sometimes to be found at the remains of an earlier area, but there are many cases of construction in secluded, remote spots. In the poetry of the time, the expression "new *ts'un*" (*hsin-ts'un*)[bg] was used frequently, and this may provide insight into the historical nature of the *ts'un*.

Following on Miyakawa's work, Miyazaki Ichisada has advanced research on this point.[29] Miyazaki sees the institution of distinct *hsiang* and *t'ing* levels as hangovers from ancient city-states. The emergence of the *ts'un*, he argues, marked the formation of the medieval village, born of the collapse of these ancient city-states. Mutual aid centering around the unit of the hamlet and its ceremonies to the "god of the soil" effectively forged bonds of solidarity between residents under the earlier system. But, in the *ts'un* system, we have to look for a new

mainstay of mutual aid, both spiritually and socially. Buddhism and Taoism, Miyazaki argues, entered the picture now as
they sought to capture men's minds.

At the same time that the "*ts'un*" phenomenon was spread-
ing, a living area known as the "*wu*" [bh] was in existence. The
compound *ts'un-wu* appears frequently, which would suggest
that, in many cases, the two terms indicated similar varieties of
population centers. We have quite a number of studies on the
wu, one of the first being the classic essay by the late Naba
Toshisada, "Ushu kō" (A study of the *wu* leader).[30] Recently,
Chin Fa-ken published a comprehensive collection of historical
materials concerning this issue.[31] From these studies, we can
put together a general picture of the *wu*.

The original meaning of the character *wu* is found in the *Tzu-
lin*[bi] (Character dictionary), cited in Li Hsien's[bj] note to the
biography of Ma Yüan[bk] in the *Hou-Han-shu*[bl] (History of the
Latter Han): a small embankment or a small wall. However, the
biography of Ma Yüan recounts that as Grand Administrator
of Lung-hsi,[bm] he memorialized for the construction of a *wu-
hou*[bn] so as to defend against raids by the Ch'iang people. In this
case, *wu* clearly denoted a military stronghold. The construction of a *wu* in this sense can also be found in the Chü-yen[bo]
wood strips of the Former Han.[32] These were installations for
border defense against the Hsiung-nu, and in the Latter Han
they were prepared particularly against Ch'iang raids. At the
time of the great Ch'iang uprising at the beginning of the second
century, it was recorded that *wu-hou* were installed in 616
strategic positions deep inland so as to link the T'ai-hang[33]
mountain range with the North China plain.

The reason for constructing *wu* was not simply as defense
against external attack, however. In times of civil war, the
general populace banded together for self-protection and what
they built were called *ying*,[bp] *pi*,[bq] and *pao*.[br] The expression *wu*
was also used in this context, the earliest example appearing
during the disorders at the end of the reign of Wang Mang.
When the Latter Han dynasty was established, the government
ordered these installations evacuated and the people returned
to agriculture.[34] During the rebellions at the end of the Latter
Han, *wu* were again set up over a wide area. Once again, during
the Yung-chia uprising of 307 under the Western Chin, the

creation of self-protective groups based on the *wu* form spread widely. As is well known, the uprising of 307 caused many Han Chinese to migrate to various areas. They moved in groups as a means of avoiding hardship, or they established *wu* at certain points where they congregated. Naba's study shows that the heads of these itinerant bands were called *hsing-chu*[bs] and the persons in charge of *wu* were called *wu-chu*.[bt]

Conditions determining the location of *wu* were in no way uniform. If we judge from the circumstances of the creation of *wu* recorded in the *Shui-ching-chu*[35] (Commentary to the *Classic of Waterways*) and elsewhere, however, it seems that there was a strong proclivity toward utilizing naturally strategic positions. For example, I-ho (unified) *wu* built near the Lo River got its name from being twenty *chang*[bu] tall, with three sides (south, north, and east) surrounded by natural bluffs, and the west side alone barricaded by manpower.[36] Also, there was reported to have been a *wu* in the Lo River basin by the name of Yün-chung wu[bv] ("amidst the clouds") because clouds and haze trailed along continuously over the steep mountains there.[37] Apparently, quite a number of *wu* were purposefully constructed in areas with natural defenses. In order to manage a group livelihood in such places, provisions for weaponry, foodstuffs, and the like were necessary. The groups planned particularly for self-sufficiency in food by cultivating the mountain lands.

It was only natural then that life in such a *wu* formed a virtually separate universe. The group life that transpired in these remote mountainous areas out of contact with the external world often stirred up images of Utopia in the imaginations of outsiders. In fact, T'ao Yüan-ming's[bw] famous work, *T'ao-hua yüan chi*[bx] (Peach Blossom Spring), is said to have been modeled on the contemporary world of a *wu*. The advocate of this theory, Ch'en Yin-k'o, argues that Tai Yen-chih,[by] who served in the army in Liu Yü's[bz] Ch'ang-an campaign in the last years of the Western Chin, explored the upper reaches of the Lo River in compliance with his orders; unable to find the river's source, he turned back midway. It was at this point, however, that he came across Po-ku *wu*,[ca] T'an-shan *wu*,[cb] and a place by the name of T'ao-yüan.[cc] Mr. Tai wrote up a report of his survey under the title *Hsi-cheng chi*[cd] (Report on the western expedition), and T'ao Yüan-ming used it as his source, Ch'en argues, for *T'ao-hua yüan chi*.[38]

In short, Ch'en's point is that *T'ao-hua yüan chi* was not simply the product of a literary imagination but was written on the basis of actual *wu* of the day. This conception leads us to the idea that the life of the people in the *wu* was a product of the desire to escape the turbulent world and preserve a peaceful society. For this reason, it was seen as a Utopia from the outside. In order for such a notion to have been conveyed, a moral order had to have been sustained among the inhabitants of the *wu*. If the *wu* had been the scene of fighting, it would not have been possible for it to preserve its life secluded from the outside world, and it surely could not have become the object of Utopian images. In the *T'ao-hua yüan chi*, the recluse Liu Lin-chih[ce] from Kiangnan learns of "T'ao-yüan" secondhand, plans to travel there, but is unable to do so because he dies of illness. "T'ao-yüan" became the object of recluse Liu's longing because it was seen both inside and out as a peaceful world free of strife.

Personal Bonds in the Wu. What sort of society was this world of the *wu* which people of the day perceived as a Utopia? Let us look at the group under T'ien Ch'ou[cf] of the Three Kingdoms era, which has frequently drawn the attention of historians in the past. Seeking revenge against enemies of his superior, T'ien Ch'ou led a group of "several hundred fellow clansmen and other dependent people" into a seclusion in the mountains of Hsü-wu[cg] (Hopei). Later, many "common folk" (*pai-hsing*)[ch] joined them until they expanded several years later into a huge band of over five thousand families.[39]

By this account, the structural components of the group were "clansmen," "dependents," and "common folk." The "dependents" have been seen as various kinds of servants, but their identity remains unclear. The "common folk" were primarily self-sufficient farmers. The *Chin-shu* (History of the state of Chin) speaks of "clansmen and commoners"[40] with respect to the structure of Yü Kun's[ci] group (late Western Chin), which I shall discuss later; and, similarly, it notes that Ch'ih Chien's[cj] group was put together by "clansmen and local people."[41] It seems from these and other examples of the *wu* structure

that the group centered around the leader's clansmen and included families with different surnames from the same local
origin, common people who came from near and far seeking
refuge, and various people of subordinate status. Hence, these
were not pure kinship groupings but included a wide variety of
non-blood-related elements. Also, the more they expanded, the
greater was this tendency.

By the time things had come to this stage, the group had
to have an established rule of order, the first requirement for
which was to decide on a group leader. Since both T'ien Ch'ou
and Yü Kun appealed for heads to be chosen for the groups,
they were themselves selected by popular demand. Other
heads of *wu* and *hsing*[ck] (itinerant groups) were selected under
similar circumstances. Worthy of note here is that *wu* and *hsing*
leaders were picked through recommendation by reputation. In
this way, people chose their own rulers, an expression of total
group unity through which people sought mutual cohesion.
Thus, in the very way the rulers were picked we can see the
nature of this group bond.

It was with this concern in mind that men of the right
character were chosen to be *wu* and *hsing* heads, and they were
men who had gained the confidence of their clansmen and
fellow villagers as a whole. This tie built on trust continued
after the formation of a refugee group. The basic impetus
bringing about such ties was the relief activities of leaders
toward their clansmen and fellow local villagers. That is, by
dividing up their personal wealth among the people in need and
thereby saving lives, these men earned a debt of gratitude from
the people. It became a common pattern for people to be deeply
respectful of such a personal quality and look up to such men
as their leaders.

Nonetheless, the reason this relief-gratitude bond could
cohere in the ruling structure of the social group cannot have
been independent of the economic conditions of the time. In the
severe famines of the day, even literati had no easy time staying
alive. In the "Biography of Ch'ih Chien"[cl] cited in the chapter
"Te-hsing"[cm] of the *Shih-shuo hsin-yü*[cn] (New sayings from the
talk of the times), it says that when the grave famine conditions
caused by the uprising of 307 struck, the possessions held by
literati and commoners were divided up to give Ch'ih Chien

something. This incident was also recorded with different phrasing in his biography in the *Chin-shu*, where it goes on to say that Ch'ih Chien divided up the resources he had received among the impoverished in his clan and local villagers.

The fact that in a time of starvation he was given provisions by an acquaintance reveals the high status held by Ch'ih Chien. By further distributing these provisions to others, he was seen as ever more personally high-minded. Thus, the act of personal sacrifice was twofold: Ch'ih Chien, the recipient of an act of individual sacrifice, becomes offerer of the same, and his biography lauds him for it. (It was precisely because of such personal qualities that Ch'ih Chien was later chosen as head of a *wu*.)

Such an act of personal sacrifice became the opportunity to bind two people spiritually, because it spawned a sense of gratitude on the part of the recipient of the act. The one who offered the relief gave up his attachment to goods in his personal possession and, in an act of *justice* (an act in compliance with the dictates of his own spirit), he roused the spirits of those he assisted and stirred up a sense of admiration among them for him.

Men who were able to transcend a position of selfishness or *profit* in this way and come to a world of *justice*, however, had to be men whose character had fulfilled this spirituality. From the past this role had been played by literati, and it was never simply by chance that leaders of the sort just described came from renowned families in their respective villages. They were practitioners as individuals of literati ethics.

Although ordinary people who lived every day under these straitened circumstances might be liable to act not from a position of *justice* but rush to one of immediate *profit*, literati by virtue of their intentions could surpass men of this nature (a hypocritical tendency among literati was born of this as well). They thus surpassed ordinary men spiritually. In their adoration for the personal qualities of such men, the common people were able to correct their own moral lives. If this inclination on the part of common men to seek profit in their daily lives had been left to its own course, conflicts of interest among the populace would have arisen everywhere and the group's livelihood would have fallen into chaos and disorder. The existence of literati leaders had the effect of suppressing this and offering an ethical order to the group.

Once T'ien Ch'ou and Yü Kun had been selected as *wu* heads, they implemented the various regulations and institutions decided upon. T'ien Ch'ou laid down over twenty items in the "Laws concerning bloodshed, violence, theft, and litigation" [co] upon which he pledged his word to the people. In addition, he instituted "Rules for marriages" [cp] and revived "Facilities for schools and instruction." [cq] Clearly, he was attempting to establish an ethico-ritual order for the life of this closed-off group in the mountains of Hsü-wu. This objective preserved the group bond and was a revenge upon the lord-servant relationship. What T'ien Ch'ou feared most was that if bloodshed and violence were stirred up among the members of the group, the group itself would fall apart and his objective would not be attained.

The same can be said in the case of Yü Kun. He advocated the need for the maintenance of morality among his group's members: "Be not reliant on forts nor seek help in disasters. Be not violent toward neighbors nor destructive of homes. Do not cut and gather wood planted by others. Seek not to act immorally nor commit an injustice. Let us bring together our physical and mental strengths and together care for those in distress." The intent here as well was to prevent the outbreak of trouble through an ethical consciousness, while preserving the existence of the group.

Once he had gained acceptance of his aims by the people, Yü Kun went to work on actual construction for the common welfare by using a natural stronghold to erect *wu* walls. It was said that: "He took into account the labor involved, devised measures, allocated labor equitably, parceled resources fairly, repaired equipment, and utilized individual capacities to the best end." The necessary realistic concern for the preservation of the group's life prompted a fairness in the labor and livelihood of the people, seen in the establishing of labor quotas and the fixing of weights and measures. In calling for the recommendations of the wisest men in each village to form a leadership structure for the group, he was carrying on a "communitarian" mode of operations for local village society and working to spread the ethico-ritual spirit throughout the entire body.

As we have seen thus far, the *wu* group of this time was never merely a cluster of refugees but a "communitarian" band centered around a virtuous leader. What made such a "communal" bond possible was the moral consciousness of each person in the group. Still, this moral consciousness was not divorced from everyday life. This was morally essential for the management of a common livelihood under the distinctive conditions of a *wu*. The group had a common political orientation, and cooperation among the members of the group was indispensable in the actual circumstances of life, such as the construction of the *wu*, forging of weapons, and securing of foodstuffs. Furthermore, since the people who gathered into such groups were not all blood-related, groups were mixtures of a variety of unrelated persons, which seems to have necessitated a strong moral awareness among the constituent members of the group.

From the picture of the *wu* as we have reconstructed it, the "communitarian" universe sought by the eremitic scholars and common people in the late Latter Han seems to have emerged in a subsequent period of convulsion and to have endured in the daily lives of people for a long period of time. While this way of life evoked an exceedingly idealized image, its ideology was indispensable for the continuance of life through such hard times. And thus the *wu* emerges with a host of different faces.

The Six Dynasties period is known as the era of the aristocracy. What then was the connection between the Six Dynasties aristocratic system and this "communitarian" universe? As noted earlier, the fact that many of the leaders of *wu* groups were of aristocratic origins with old or great surnames offers one suggestion for dealing with this issue. In the next section, I should like to focus directly on the issue of the aristocracy.

The Autonomous World of the Six Dynasties Aristocracy

The Social Base of the Six Dynasties Aristocracy. As discussed earlier, the structure of Wei-Chin society differed from that of the ancient period in that it took form on the basis of qualitatively new "communitarian" relations. These social bonds should then have been operative throughout the aristocratic system established in this period. In this section, I should like to verify such a prediction.

What was it that gave form to the Six Dynasties aristocracy as a ruling class in this period? Many people have already pointed out the difficulties involved in seeing a manorial system or a large landownership system as necessary preconditions for this aristocracy. It is more appropriately regarded as a bureaucratic aristocracy or an aristocracy of culture than as a landed aristocracy. I agree that this is undoubtedly true as an expression of the *form* of the Six Dynasties aristocratic ruling class. But, I feel that two questions have yet to be thoroughly investigated: (1) If we call them a bureaucratic aristocracy, does that imply that their essence as a class was merely as servants to the emperor? and (2) If we call them an aristocracy of culture, what was their relationship to contemporary society?[42] In short, the unresolved problem remains the class basis of the Six Dynasties aristocracy.

There is more to it than this, though, for the very importance of this problem has apparently not been realized as yet. More generally, the issue is one of how class relations existed without the direct mediation of relations of ownership over the means of production. Thus, it would seem as though this may offer an important hint for explaining the distinctive structure of Chinese history. For this reason, I have in recent years asserted the existence of a medieval "community" at the basis of Six Dynasties society, and I have discussed the logical structure of this assertion in other writings.[43] Still, much of the criticism of colleagues regarding my work has disappointed me. They cling stubbornly to their own historical views, and few seem aware of the need for flexible thought in which an understanding of Chinese history is not trapped in preconceptions. In other words, they fail to recognize how postwar studies of Chinese history have become miserably bungled because of a lack of such thought.[44]

To summarize the points thus far raised in connection with this issue,[45] the literati ethic of self-restraint toward worldly desires (wealth and power) brought into existence a "communitarian" cohesiveness in family, patrilineage, and local village— the literati universe. Personal evaluations or *hsiang-lun*[cr] (evaluation based on local reputation) which revolved around this ethic provided the qualifications for leadership in society. The class position of the Six Dynasties aristocracy was grounded in this *hsiang-lun* and served as the base for their autonomous status vis à vis dynastic authority.

The ruling structure of the Six Dynasties aristocracy—I shall be looking particularly at the Northern Dynasties—clearly possessed the shared pattern of a "communitarian" bond centered on a moral intelligentsia, as seen in the Taoist and *wu* groupings. A new orientation toward "community" which becomes evident in the late Latter Han was systematized as the Six Dynasties aristocratic system. More to the point, it was the aristocratic stratum in the Six Dynasties which, riding the crest of this orientation, established itself as a ruling class. The most concrete, structural manifestation of their institutionalization was the Nine Ranks recruitment system for the bureaucracy.

The Six Dynasties aristocracy were superintendents of the moral "community." For people familiar with a historical conception of development modeled on European history, this view may seem exceedingly idealized, but if we are to address the actualities of China's distinctive civil bureaucratic society directly and try to clarify its structure—at the intellectual center of which were Confucian principles—then we must trace the points of contact between this spirit and society. Furthermore, this was not simply a world of ideas. The class basis for the Six Dynasties aristocracy did not form as a direct function of material means but existed at a level in which this was transcended by the spiritual realm. By spiritual realm is meant not simply the universe originally enjoyed by individual aristocrats but the real human relations that brought together an ethically based society (social contacts within family, patrilineage, and local village, and among literati). Here was the essence of the society supporting this aristocratic class as rulers, and it was the essence of this society that enabled the Six Dynasties aristocracy to gain autonomy as a ruling class.

Spurred by the aristocratic spirit, this society formed the foundation that gave clear expression to itself. The antinomian positions of the side spurring and the side being acted on met here, and their synthesis composed "aristocratic society." The aristocratic class was able to achieve autonomy from dynastic authority by being supported by this world. Simultaneously, they enjoyed an independent existence in the formation of this world itself. The aristocracy's spiritual work on behalf of the objective world was not offered merely to gain popularity in public opinion—or even a good post in the bureaucracy. I cannot claim that such a utilitarian conscious-ness was totally absent, for it was characteristic of the Chinese not to lapse into an excessive fastidiousness with respect to utilitarianism. However, it seems likely that this spiritual world originally existed among the aristocracy, and the spiritual realm of the Six Dynasties aristocracy existed in a profound way as an issue in their lives. We need to penetrate this internal uni-verse if we are to recognize the strong class autonomy of the Six Dynasties aristocracy and locate its foundation in the moral "community" created by the relations between them and the people.

The Spirit of Transcending the Mundane. When we examine the spiritual way of life of the Six Dynasties aristocracy, we cannot assess it simply as asceticism, as several examples may demonstrate. Ts'ui Po-ch'ien[cs] of Po-ling[ct] was satisfied to live according to the "way of refinement" (*ya-tao*)[cu] and refused to have contact with or seek advancement from Ts'ui Hsien,[cv] a younger member of his clan, who was a powerful official of the Eastern Wei court.[46]

Then there was Lu I-hsi[cw] of Fan-yang[cx] who, at the end of the Northern Wei, for many years remained in a leisurely sinecure and retained a nonchalant attitude. When urged to meet with important officials and request advancement, he refused, saying: "I have learned the way of the former kings, and I revere the implementation of their will. Why need I seek any wealth and fame at all?"[47]

There is also the following anecdote about Lu. The court favorite of the Empress Ling,[cy] Li Shen-kuei,[cz] sought the hand of Lu's daughter in marriage, but Lu rejected the offer and married her into another family. Upon hearing this, the Em-press dispatched a secret imperial messenger on the night of the wedding with an order to stop the ceremony. Undaunted, Lu I-hsi showed no sign of being upset. Were he to have sought wealth or glory by any means, then forging a marriage liaison with such an influential man would surely have been a shortcut. At the time, the end of the Northern Wei, such a trend had become rather general. However, Lu was too proud to "seek any wealth and fame at all" and wanted to live according to the "way of the former kings." The case of Ts'ui Po-ch'ien was the same. Rather than follow the authorities in power and pursue personal distinction, he chose to live peacefully in his own world with the "way of refinement."

As these common examples describe, glory in the bureaucratic world was not necessarily the one and only way of life for concerned aristocrats. The reason they did not boldly pursue their own advancement was not simply out of moral propriety but because they considered it most important that a realm that sustained their attitudes toward life exist and that they live in it. This realm was the "way of refinement" for Ts'ui and the "way of the former kings" for Lu; for both we might call it the realm of the "way" (*tao*).[da] This was a spiritual realm transcending the mundane world, as the term "way of refinement" aptly expressed. Primary for these people was dependency on it and life within it. It would seem that because they possessed this spiritual realm within themselves, they could achieve a freedom from having their minds trapped in the affairs of the mundane world.

What actually constituted this spiritual realm that I have just dubbed the realm of the "way?" Looking again at Lu I-hsi's words, we see that he did not deny wealth and fame in and of themselves. He was too proud to "seek any wealth and fame at all," or to keep after men in authority and gain wealth and fame with their help. For Lu, the position of wealth and fame ought to have been the result of having "learned the way of the former kings and having implemented their will." He considered that a desire for wealth and power which dispensed with these basic principles was shameful for a scholarly man. In this conception, it was the interiority of a human being—his learning and its application—that had to determine that person's social position. And no external element could be vital in the establishment of that position.

The notion that the political position of the aristocracy had to be this way was not limited to Lu I-hsi. The family of Li Hsiao-chen[db] of Chao-chün,[dc] who served the Northern Ch'i court, repeatedly formed marriage relations with the imperial household, beginning with his female cousin who became empress to Emperor Wen-hsüan[dd] (r. 550–560). Li's brothers both had attained success through their own literary talents and were embarrassed by the fact that they were [now] maternal relatives."[48]

Also, there was a fascinating exchange between Wei Shou[de] (author of the *Wei-shu*) and Ts'ui Ling[df] (from a famous clan in Ch'ing-ho prefecture). Although the two men had been at odds for some time, when Wei as an emissary to the state of Liang passed through Hsü-chou, Ts'ui (the governor of Hsü-chou) sallied forth in a state procession of great pomp to meet him and had another man address Wei: "Fear not the many ceremonial bodyguards; there is strength in cultivation." And Wei responded: "Tell Ts'ui of Hsü-chou that perhaps there is merit in raising troops, perhaps there is some cultivation involved." Always proud of his pedigree, Ts'ui became extremely angry upon hearing these words.[49]

Ts'ui was a man who had reached a high position in the Eastern Wei state through meritorious service at the time Kao Huan[dg] had raised an army (to quell a rebellion against the throne). Wei Shou pointed out that Ts'ui's position as governor of Hsü-chou owed nothing to cultivated learning, and ridiculed him for having gotten it by depending on men in power.

As these two examples demonstrate, the aristocracy of the period were proud of having attained their political positions not by relying on the powers that be but through their cultured talents (cultivation), in which they had trained themselves in literature and scholarship. Wei's aloofness from Ts'ui's mundane concerns represents a common notion among the aristocracy then. There is a certain thread connecting Lu I-hsi's and Ts'ui Po-ch'ien's rejection of "seeking any wealth and fame at all" with the realm of the "way" in which they sought to live. In other words, the notion that a human being's position in society should be based of necessity on this internal realm is common to these cases. Also, it was implicitly clear that learning gave expression to this internal realm as knowledge. In short, it is no exaggeration to say that cultivated learning was what enabled the Six Dynasties aristocracy to have autonomy as a ruling class. This supports the view, mentioned earlier, of a cultivated aristocracy, but we must go on to ask what was meant by "learning" as the intellectual expression of the internal realm of the aristocracy.

The Meaning of Learning for the Six Dynasties Aristocracy. Yen Chih-t'ui[du] has the following to say in his *Yen-shih chia-hsün* (Family instructions for the Yen clan).[50]

People do not always have the support of a family or local village. If forced into exile, they would have no one to protect them and would have to look out for themselves. The most appropriate skill with which to be equipped under such circumstances, Yen argued, was book learning. This was Yen Chih-t'ui's perception of learning, acquired through the lengthy experience of having tasted the bitterness of wandering from the states of Liang to Northern Chou,[di] and on to Northern Ch'i,[dj] and from there back to Northern Chou, and on to Sui.[dk] For Yen, a literatus in search of the final authority upon which to base his life would find it not in the family or in the local village but in the learning he acquired for himself.

Yen's view of learning reflected a social trend of that time when the system of a pedigreed aristocracy was rapidly declining. As Yoshikawa Tadao has noted, one pervasive feature of that time was a belief in a principle that stressed the importance of men of ability.[51] However, the origin of the aristocratic system, in the last analysis, was neither the clan nor the local village, but in fact the very learning cultivated by literati— namely, their autonomous spirit. This point needs further study, but Yen Chih-t'ui's words speak to the value of knowledge of books as a way to make a living. What, after all, was the true objective of book learning or scholarship?

Yen Chih-t'ui gave the following answer to this question: "The reason for reading and studying is primarily to open one's mind and clarify one's vision in order to benefit one's conduct."[52] In other words, the significance of reading and scholarship was that they enabled people to live their lives through the development of knowledge. Yen criticized well-read men who did not live in a fashion corresponding to their learning, and he stressed that knowledge of books should be linked to practice. Yet how are knowledge and practice connected? Yen argued that men who had not behaved in a filial manner toward their parents would learn through books of the deeds of past men who had served their parents devotedly, reflect on themselves and feel a strong sense of shame, and then resolve to act in accordance with prescriptions of filiality.

And this learning would apply not only to parental obedience. Men who had not known to serve a lord would learn from the loyal acts of past men, reflect on themselves, and resolve to sacrifice themselves in allegiance. Men who had been profligate would study the ethics of humility exemplified in the actions of past men and ponder living that way themselves. Men who had originally been miserly and avaricious would learn, through the deeds of past men, of the generosity of stressing justice, self-restraint, and charity; and then they would strive for these ends themselves. Similarly, men of violence would learn from men of the past the commendable morality of tolerance and change their earlier attitudes; while cowards, inspired by the bravery of past men, would seek to live their lives with courage.

Yen lists many other objectives to learning, but the idea he expressed was that one would realize through the actions of the ancients that one was not living as befit one's character and, through a profound, penetrating self-reflection, take a step to putting such a life into practice. Thus, knowledge was transformed into action through a kind of mental conversion.

What gave rise to this conversion that mediated knowledge and action? Clearly, it was the result of realizing one's immorality in comparison with the ethical behavior of the ancients. If we delve a little deeper into this opposition between morality and immorality, we find a fundamental difference over what constitutes a human being, for a spirit of selflessness impelled men to act morally and egotism impelled men to immorality. For example, in order for filiality—acting in a devoted manner to one's parents—to come into existence, the individuality of the child had to be obliterated. Loyalty to state and sovereign resembled this. Surely, there were a variety of ways of expressing this spirit of selflessness when it came to humility, stressing justice over wealth, self-restraint, giving charity, and acting tolerantly. Also, courage was itself the result of transcending egotism. The moral actions of the ancients were permeated with this spirit of selflessness. In contrast to the pure and noble character of such men, the self was merely the spokesman of a narrow egotism in one's relationship with parents, sovereign, and others. Thus, one became aware of a fierce sense of shame before this degeneration of a selfish humanity which this comparison illuminated. And, on the basis of a change of heart, the determination to put morality into practice was born.

The aim of reading and learning for Yen Chih-t'ui, as we

have seen, was to awaken men to pursue moral and righteous ways through self-reflection. This conversion was an awakening to one's own ignominious bearing, illuminated by the moral acts of past men and cooped up in one's egotism. Thus, "learning" for Yen also possessed a religious nature; or, rather, it was not limited merely to a conception of learning. In the words of Lu I-hsi, whom we met earlier—"I have learned the way of the former kings, and I revere the implementation of their will. Why need I seek any wealth and fame at all?"—learning is also connected directly to practice, and Lu was attempting to transcend the realm of selfishness inherent in "seeking any wealth and fame at all." I have already referred to this as the universe of the "way," a kind of transcendent spiritual realm. The intellectual structure supporting and legitimizing it was learning. This was both the learning of ethical norms and an understanding of history as indicated by the practices of "the ancients" who bequeathed "the way of the former kings." Hence, it was not simply an abstracted metaphysics.

The importance of learning for the Six Dynasties aristocracy may now be a bit clearer. The selfless spirit of the aristocracy became a daily ethic in their appeal to the world around them. It formed the pivot for "communitarian" cohesion in the outside world, and it was learning that nurtured this spirit. In other words, literati learning at that time can be seen as an intellectual system aimed at human education. The ethical activities of the Six Dynasties aristocracy carried on the long and rich tradition of scholarship centered on the classics. Hence, this scholarship was conducted and accumulated with a focus on the realization of the moral "communitarian" realm in Chinese society. The literati, the aristocracy of the day, mediated this learning for society.

Generally, the Six Dynasties aristocracy may be called men of learning, like Yen Chih-t'ui. The famous clans of the Northern dynasties such as Ts'ui, Lu, Li, and Cheng each produced formidable scholars of great erudition. We cannot list each and every one of them, but in the biography of Li Tzu-hsiung[dl] from Chao-chün it says: "Although his family had for generations established itself through scholarship, Li Tzu-hsiung alone studied equestrianism and archery. His elder brother Tzu-tan[dm] called him to task for this, saying 'to discard the word (*wen*)^{dn} and revere the sword (*wu*)^{do} is no way for a literatus to be.'"[53] Thus, learning itself was not only the indispensable grounding for a literatus but also a family occupation by which one established oneself with each generation.

To say that learning served as the existential basis for the aristocracy may not be an exaggeration. The fount of the qualifications befitting a leader in society lay in his personal qualities, and what nurtured these qualities was in fact learning. The basic significance of the point that the Six Dynasties aristocracy was an aristocracy of culture should now be apparent. Private ownership of the means of production did not directly establish their social position. Rather, transcending the direct control over the means of production, it was grounded in their being leaders who integrated a society structured around individual owners. Their leadership was accordingly intellectual and moral, and learning served an indispensable function in ruling the people.

In order to clarify the meaning of learning in this context more fully, we have to examine what it actually entailed, but that cannot be done here. If I might add one word though, the essential point for literati learning was of course its moral scope, and thus classical scholarship was of central importance. Yet the *Yen-shih chia-hsün* deplored the fact that learned men of the day lacked knowledge of jurisprudence and civil administration, to say nothing of their ignorance of architecture or agriculture, and incurred the ridicule of military men and petty functionaries. Literati learning actually included knowledge for practical learning of this sort.

A look through the biographies of Northern aristocrats shows that the learning they attained—*yin-yang*, astronomy, mathematics, the calendar, medicine, divination, and prediction based on the direction and sound of the winds—while not necessarily orthodox, did include fields in the life sciences. However, we also find the metaphysics of Taoism and Buddhism, as well as literature as a form of expressionism. As noted earlier, learning was itself a form of historical understanding, and with the development of genealogical study, historiography at this time pioneered its own distinctive field. Thus, at the mountain peak of learning stood classical scholarship, and at its foot was an extremely broad mixture of metaphysical and material fields that seemed to form an expansive system. While this composed the intellectual basis for transcendence by the Six Dynasties aristocracy, it was also the source for praxis in the objective world.

Why did a cultured aristocracy established on the basis of learning result in a system of pedigree? "Learning" was an activity aimed at the formation of acquired character. I have not yet worked out fully my own ideas on this issue, but as we have seen, the intellectual system of that time did not exist simply as objective knowledge but seems to have been an embodiment of an exceptional personalism or transcendence. Thus, if one recognized the need for human qualities to match a mastery of learning, then might this not usher in a status system of pedigree?

There is an inescapable contradiction here, however. One's acquired nature, which is ancillary to learning, conflicts with the innate qualities of a wise man. The emergence of the principle of laying stress on men of talent as opposed to that of pedigree was a necessary process in this sense. That the cultured aristocracy would eventually spawn an examination system should be seen as a natural conclusion. Yen Chih-t'ui's bitterness in decrying the ignorant ways of high-born sons who had earned the ridicule of military men and petty officials ought to indicate negatively the inseparable link between the Six Dynasties aristocratic system and learning.

The States of the Northern Dynasties, Sui, and T'ang, and the "Community" Ethic

The Han Chinese Aristocracy and the Regimes of the Five Barbarians and the Northern Wei. We have thus far concentrated our discussion on the autonomy of the Han Chinese aristocracy as a ruling class in North China. Now we need to delve more deeply into the history of their relationship to state power. Under the regimes of the "Five Barbarians"—non-Chinese peoples of the Northern dynasties—their position as a ruling class was not fully established in the political sense. Especially from the period of the Five Barbarians through the first half of the Northern Wei, the state was organized in a dual Han-barbarian structure in which each race was put under a respective ruling system. The non-Chinese peoples still retained the vestiges of their tribal "community" from the era when they had lived outside China's borders; this was particularly evident in the changes in the organization of their military, which made up the core of state power.[54]

When a state so heavily colored by its alien rulers came to rule the North China plain, it encompassed Han society under its control. The aristocrats who were the leaders in Han society naturally were appointed as officials. Some of these officials of aristocratic origin were active in central politics and on occasion became leaders of state, enjoying the full confidence of the sovereign. Examples would include Chang Pin[dp] under Shih Lo[dq] [274–333, founder of the Latter Chao[dr] dynasty], Wang Meng[ds] under Fu Chien[dt] [338–385, head of the Former Ch'in],[du] and Ts'ui Hung[dv] and Ts'ui Hao[dw] (father and son) in the early years of the Northern Wei. Many Han Chinese aristocrats became high or subordinate officials in their native districts and spent their lives in their local villages.

The bureaucratization of Han aristocrats, however, did not mean that they participated in state power in a completely subjective manner, for sovereignty remained in the hands of the non-Chinese. The "slip of the pen" incident involving Ts'ui Hao, which occurred during the reign of Emperor T'ai-wu[dx] [r. 424–452] of the Northern Wei, made this realization bitterly clear for Han aristocrats. The incident originated when the Northern Wei national history being written by Ts'ui Hao and others incurred the animosity of the aliens. It was said that Ts'ui had been actively maneuvering to reorganize the Northern Wei into an aristocratic state, and this invited a barbarian reaction. As is well known, along with the steady progress made in the unification of North China in the time of Emperor T'ai-wu, Han aristocrats entered political circles in large numbers. The absolute confidence that the Emperor T'ai-wu placed in Ts'ui Hao caused the illusion to arise that a barbarian regime was now apparently being transformed into a Han-style aristocratic state. As a result, Ts'ui was executed (in 450) and those implicated extended to the Ts'ui family and the Shantung aristocratic families related by marriage to them.

As this indicated, the political discrimination of barbarian and Han was strictly enforced in the unified Northern Wei state.

The political role of the barbarians in the Northern Wei state was primarily military. Troops at the center and in the localities consisted mostly of soldiers of barbarian roots. To non-Chinese fighters who achieved military successes there opened the road to civil officialdom. This point would lead one to believe that the structure of the state, at least in an overall sense, was not formed by an aristocratic system.

In the dozen or so years after T'ai-wu was assassinated by the eunuch Tsung Ai,[dy] bloodly secret feuds occurred within the Northern Wei imperial court. In this interval there was no external expansion. By the time Emperor Hsien-wen[dz] [r. 466–471] had succeeded in annexing the Shantung region, it seems that the extent of contact between the Northern Wei state and Northern Chinese society was considerably deepened. Emperor Hsiao-wen's[ea] [r. 471–500] decisive moving of the capital to Lo-yang thereafter was apparently a result of these conditions, for earlier the government had inaugurated policies for structuring the agricultural society of North China. We see this in the early years of Hsiao-wen's reign when the Empress Wen-ming[eb] held control of the government with the creation of the "three chiefs" (*san-chang*)[ec] and equitable field (*chün-t'ien*)[ed] systems. These policies may reveal the connections at the time between the barbarian regime and the Han Chinese aristocrats.

The Equitable Field System and Aristocratic Ethics. The view has recently gained favor of looking at the equitable field system as an extension of the system of per capita land allocation (*chi-k'ou shou-t'ien*),[ee] which flourished in the years of the unification wars under Emperor T'ai-wu.[55] My own view differs in no way from the notion of a linkage in the history of agricultural management policy of the Northern Wei state between per capita land allocation and the equitable field system. But the problem lies in what meaning we are to attach to this linkage. Many commentators have understood this as a state policy flexing its external muscles vis à vis Han aristocrats (and hence a policy to repress the Han aristocracy). There is also the position that sees this as a distinctly non-Chinese policy. What view are we to assume? Clearly, behind the system of per capita land allotment lay a policy for handling a conquered people under state power, known as the relocation policy. The equitable field system itself was a kind of policy to limit land ownership with the premise of state intervention. It can be assumed that the functions of this state power gave rise to these earlier perspectives, but this is still a rather simplistic understanding of the problem.

With the relocation policy that lay behind the system of per capita land allotment, the state moved the conquered people to strategic environs near the capital and put into effect centralized control over these areas. The per capita land allotment system supplied land to people in accordance with the labor power possessed by the migrant populace and looked toward the establishment of a self-cultivating peasantry as the basic structure for Han society. The principle of the equitable field system shared this conception in that "the land is to be used by all and no man will be idle." When we examine the essence of these conceptions, a linkage is forged with the broad world of the self-managing peasantry.

The reconstruction of this world had been a problem since the time of Tung Chung-shu in the Former Han. Its aims through the policy to limit large landholdings had always ended in failure throughout the Han. A new characteristic from the Three Kingdoms on was to limit large landholdings and, as well, to institute a land allocation policy for the small peasantry. The linkage from "military colonies" (*t'un-t'ien*),[ef] to "lands in possession" (*chan-t'ien*) and "assessment lands" (*k'e-t'ien*),[56] to the equitable field system testifies to this effect. The per capita land allotment system also, without a doubt, formed one part of this lineage.

What sort of social class gave rise to this string of policies? We know only that the name of the man who designed the equitable field system was Li An-shih,[eg] and we cannot overlook the fact that he came from the famous Li clan of Chao-chün. If we accept the view that the Six Dynasties aristocracy were large landowners, then we face a logical contradiction in that policies for limitations on large landholdings, like the equitable field system, were initiated by this very aristocracy. As we have seen thus far, however, the class base of the Six Dynasties aristocracy was not to be directly found here. Rather, it lay in an ethical bond with a society in which the self-managing peasantry were the backbone of the agricultural village. In other words, there was a mutual relationship between the moral ties of the aristocracy to the outside world and the societal reputation produced thereby. Aristocrats who did have large land-holdings were deeply troubled for falling into rivalries with the self-cultivating peasants (contesting the people for profit), for they were supposed to function as an organ of relief for the people. The stress on justice over wealth, which was the proper literati bearing—namely, the life ethic of frugality, self-restraint, relief, and disinterest in one's own property—was not unconnected to landownership.

Thus, the principles of the equitable field system and the concept of landownership in the aristocratic ethic did not contradict each other but even shared a certain spirit. What were these large landholdings that the equitable field system tried to restrain? It was management over large tracts of land aimed at expanding the extravagances and profits of large landowners. This management established competitive relations with the self-cultivating peasantry and wiped them out, causing a polarization of the annexers and the propertyless. This circumstance not only ran contrary to the literati ethic but it also gave birth to an unbalanced relationship between land and labor power, resulting in an irrational state economy.

To say that those responsible for managing large landholdings did not include aristocrats would be an exaggeration. Cases in which the aristocratic class forgot the literati ethic on which it was founded and sought personal economic profit were not rare. Furthermore, this trend seems to have been rather closely linked to a tendency toward stabilizing the position of the aristocracy with the development of a system of pedigree. Gradually, they moved away from their original class base.

The equitable field system may then be seen as the original economic ethic of the aristocracy being systematized as a state land law under the state control of a barbarian people. In short, at the stage prior to Emperor Hsiao-wen's policy for aristocratic pedigree, there was ample room for the implementation of joint Han-barbarian government on the basis of this common principle.

The Base Structure of the Sui-T'ang Reunification. The "sinification" policy during the period of Emperor Hsiao-wen's personal rule, however, aimed at changing the very nature of the state. With the withdrawal of earlier racial discrimination, the state attempted to organize a bureaucratic structure by differentiating scholars and commoners. Thus, the aristocratic system permeated state power, and the influence of Southern dynastic pedigrees was strongly felt as a consequence. The Han aristocracy adhered to state power, which completed the institutionalization of the aristocracy. The ruling position of the aristocratic class was guaranteed and fixed by the power of the state. Yet, in one regard this caused a deterioration of the aristocracy. Characteristic of the years after Hsiao-wen's reign were many cases where a decline in the literati ethic caused public rebuke of Han aristocrats.

Hsiao-wen's policy, though, proved unable conclusively to make the Han aristocracy bear the brunt of state power, for at this same time the main military force remained officers and troops of non-Chinese stock. Thus, when the Han aristocracy gained a preeminent political position, the non-Chinese military men were faced with a basic dilemma. Military service had carried with it the honor of being the cornerstone of the state; it had opened up opportunities for bureacratic advancement. But now, it only meant being a running dog of the Han Chinese aristocracy.

I have already discussed in detail elsewhere[57] how the explosion of this dilemma brought about the revolt of the central imperial guard and the uprising of the Six Commanderies, caused riots of the military households attached to the commanderies, and brought about the dissolution of the Northern Wei. When these uprisings occurred, the Han aristocrats tried to defend their positions by organizing militarily with local villagers. As noted earlier, the relationship between them and the local people (local militias) might best be seen as having made the everyday relationship of aristocrat and villager function militarily now. Thus, when the aristocratic class could no longer rely on the regime, they tried to confront the crisis with a latent power which they still held. The "communitarian" universe that formed the base structure for medieval Chinese society once again revealed itself quite clearly now.

As this development became institutionalized as a state structure, we can see its main traits. The *fu-ping*^{eh} (militia) system of the Western Wei, formed with the strong base of local blocs, provided the military backbone subsequently for the Northern Chou, Sui, and T'ang states, and demonstrated its tremendous might in the task of reunifying China. It had a qualitatively similar importance to the equitable field system, created with the principle of the aristocratic ethic in mind, which systematized agricultural management of these later unified states.

In order for the state institutionalization of the aristocratic ethic to be realized, there were generated various changes within the social structure of aristocratic rule. To describe this new type of aristocracy oriented toward these changes, I have used such expressions as the principle of stress on talent, new aristocratism, and enlightened aristocratism.[58] This new trend can be seen as well in the structure of these local militia bands, but of course this whole trend was later institutionalized in the examination system from the Sui dynasty onward.

Thus far, scholars have understood the flow toward China's reunification, which takes its source from the later Northern Dynasties, as the power of the state keeping the aristocrats down. No clear answer has been given to the question of the class nature of the ruling structure of this state. My own view on the Sui-T'ang empire comes back to the point that "communitarian" society of both Han and barbarian merged through mutual penetration and created a state based on these new aristocratic principles. This was a crystallization of the medieval "community" and in this sense may be regarded as the fulfillment of the medieval state. The direct root form of this completed state was the Western Wei and Northern Chou. The principle of the Western Wei's "Liu-t'iao chao-shu"[ei] (Edict of six articles) vividly indicated how the state worked to diffuse through itself the aristocratic ethos.[59]

Glossary to Part II

a	宗法	af	師丹
b	士族	ag	孔光
c	国	ah	王莽
d	子産	ai	桓
e	鄭	aj	梁
f	管仲	ak	靈
g	斉	al	楊聯陞
h	宗族	am	濁流
i	郷党	an	門生故吏
j	父老	ao	党錮
k	父兄	ap	名士
l	子弟	aq	申屠蟠
m	郷	ar	袁閎
n	亭	as	浮華交会
o	県	at	胡三省
p	郡	au	太学
q	郷三老	av	登龍門
r	県三老	aw	竇武
s	郡三老	ax	竇遊平
t	国三老	ay	陳垣
u	陳勝	az	通鑑胡注表微
v	劉邦	ba	浮華
w	士	bb	偽善
x	武	bc	社
y	郷挙里選	bd	義舍
z	董仲舒	be	村
aa	孝廉	bf	坊
ab	秦始皇帝	bg	新村
ac	南越	bh	塢
ad	氐	bi	字林
ae	羌	bj	李賢

bk 馬援

bl 後漢書

bm 隴西太守

bn 塢候

bo 居延

bp 營

bq 壁

br 保

bs 行主

bt 塢主

bu 丈

bv 雲中

bw 陶淵明

bx 桃花源記

by 戴延之

bz 劉裕

ca 百谷塢

cb 檀山塢

cc 桃源

cd 西征記

ce 劉驎之

cf 田疇

cg 徐無

ch 百姓

ci 庾袞

cj 郗鑒

ck 郗鑒別伝

cl 行

cm 德行

cn 世説新語

co 相殺傷犯盜靜訟之法

cp 婚姻嫁娶之礼

cq 学校講授之業

cr 鄉論

cs 崔伯謙

ct 博陵

cu 雅道

cv 崔暹

cw 盧義僖

cx 范陽

cy 靈

cz 李神軌

da 道

db 李孝貞

dc 趙郡

dd 文宣帝

de 魏收

df 崔悛

dg 高歡

dh 顔之推

di 北周

dj 北斉

dk 隋

dl 李子雄

dm 子旦

dn 文

do 武

dp 張賓

dq 石勒

dr 後趙

ds 王猛

dt 苻堅

du 前秦

dv 崔宏

dw 崔浩

dx 太武

dy 宗愛

dz 献文

ea 孝文

eb 文明

ec 三長

ed 均田

ee 計口授田

ef 屯田

eg 李安世

eh 府兵

ei 六条詔書

Notes to Part II

1. Wang Kuo-wei 王国維, "Yin-Chou chih-tu lun" 殷周制度論 (On Shang and Chou institutions), in *Kuan-t'ang chi-lin* 觀堂集林 (*chuan* 10), in *Wang Kuo-wei hsien-sheng ch'üan-chi* 王国維先生全集 (Collected works of Wang Kuo-wei), Taipei: T'ai-wan ta-t'ung shu-chü, 1976, vol. 2, pp. 449–478.

2. Naitō Konan 内藤湖南, *Shina jōkoshi* 支那上古史 (Ancient Chinese history), in *Naitō Konan zenshū* 内藤湖南全集 (Collected works of Naitō Konan), Chikuma shobō, 1969, Vol. X, pp. 68–70.

3. Kaizuka Shigeki 貝塚茂樹, *Chūgoku kodai shigaku no hatten* 中国古代史学の発展, Kōbundō shobō, 1946, pp. 335f.

4. Masubuchi Tatsuo 増淵龍夫, "Shunjū Sengoku jidai no shakai to kokka" 春秋戦国時代の社会と国家 (Society and state in the Spring and Autumn and Warring States periods), in *Iwanami kōza sekai rekishi 4: kodai 4* 岩波講座世界歴史 4：古代 4 (Iwanami's history of the world 4: Antiquity 4), Iwanami shoten, 1970, pp. 139–184.

5. *Lun-yü* 論語 (Analects of Confucius), "Yen-yüan" 顔淵, XI.2. Translation follows James Legge, *The Chinese Classics*, Hong Kong: Hong Kong University Press, 1966, Vol. I, p. 256. (JAF)

6. Tanigawa, "Chūgoku shi no sekai shi teki ha'aku wa dō susunda ka (1): Kodai shakai no seikaku ronsō o megutte" 中国史の世界史的把握はどう進んだか（1）：古代社会の性格論争をめじって (How has our understanding of Chinese history in world history progressed (1)? On the debate over the nature of ancient society), *Rekishi hyōron* 歴史評論 184 (December 1965), pp. 30–36; included under the title, "Chūgoku kodai shakai no seikaku ronsō: Doreisei kara kyōdōtai e" 中国古代社会の性格論争：奴隷制から共同体へ (The debate over the nature of ancient Chinese society, from slavery to "community"), in Tanigawa, *Chūgoku chūsei shakai to kyōdōtai* 中国中世社会と共同体 (Medieval Chinese society and "community"), Kokusho kankōkai, 1976, pp. 136–146.

7. See. for example, Utsunomiya Kiyoyoshi 宇都宮清吉, "Chūgoku kodai chūsei shi ha'aku no tame no ichi shikaku" 中国古代中世史把握のための一視角 (One view toward an understanding of ancient and medieval Chinese history), in *Chūgoku chūsei shi kenkyū: Rikuchō Zui Tō no shakai to bunka* 中国中世史研究：六朝隋唐の社会と文化 (Studies in medieval Chinese history: Society and culture in the Six Dynasties, Sui, and T'ang), edited by Chūgoku chūsei shi kenkyūkai 中国中世史研究会 (Society for the study of medieval Chinese history), Tōkai University Press, 1970, pp. 17–39. Reprinted in Utsunomiya, *Chūgoku kodai chūsei shi kenkyū* 中国古代中世史研究 (Studies in ancient and medieval Chinese history), Sōbunsha, 1977, pp. 3–29.

8. 三族. See Ch'ü T'ung-tsu, *Han Social Structure*, Seattle: University of Washington Press, 1967, p. 251 n.1. (JAF)

9. See Tanigawa essay cited in note 6.

10. Utsunomiya also claims that the autonomous world (sustained by this

130   *Medieval Period in China*

family system) matured into a society of great clans and produced the next epoch of the Six Dynasties period. One of the characteristics of his understanding of Chinese history is a powerless world existing at the opposite end of the spectrum from the world of power and control. My own conception of "community" relies heavily on Utsunomiya's work.

11. 里 . Translations for some of the Han period terminology (as in this case) follow Hans Bielenstein, *The Bureaucracy of Han Times*, Cambridge: Cambridge University Press, 1980. (JAF)

12. *Shih-chi* 史記, *chuan* 8, "Kao-tsu pen-chi" 高祖本紀 (Basic annals of Kao-tsu). See Burton Watson, trans., *Records of the Grand Historian of China*, New York and London: Columbia University Press, 1961, vol. 1, p. 82, for a slightly different translation. (JAF)

13. Ibid. See Watson, p. 90. Liu Pang's Three Articles were: (1) murder was punishable by death; (2) injury and theft were punishable; and (3) all the other complex and harsh Ch'in laws were abolished. (JAF)

14. Moriya Mitsuo 守屋美都雄, "Furō" 父老 (Elders), *Tōyōshi kenkyū* 東洋史研究 14.1–2 (July 1955), pp. 43–60; included in his *Chūgoku kodai no kazoku to kokka* 中国古代の家族と国家 (Family and the state in ancient China), Kyoto, Tōyōshi kenkyūkai, 1968, pp. 191–213.

15. Naitō Konan, *Shina jōkoshi*, p. 11.

16. See Tanigawa, *Zui-Tō teikoku keisei shiron* 隋唐帝国形成史論 (A historical analysis of the formation of the Sui-T'ang empire), Chikuma shobō, 1971, section I.

17. 清流, signifying a purity of criticism offered by men of learning. (JAF)

18. Kawakatsu Yoshio 川勝義雄, "Shina chūsei kizoku seiji no seiritsu ni tsuite" シナ中世貴族政治の成立について (On the establishment of aristocratic politics in medieval China), *Shirin* 史林 33.4 (August 1950), pp. 47–63; included in his *Rikuchō kizokusei shakai no kenkyū* 六朝貴族制社会の研究 (Studies of aristocratic society in the Six Dynasties period), Iwanami shoten, 1982.

19. *Yüeh-tan-p'ing* 月旦評 in Chinese; a practice begun by Hsü Shao 許劭 of the Han, who spent the first day of each month engaged in the writing of criticisms of the world around him. (JAF)

20. Masubuchi Tatsuo 増淵龍夫, "Go-Kan tōko jiken no shihyō ni tsuite" 後漢党錮事件の史評について(On the historical evaluation of the repression of cliques in the Latter Han), *Hitotsubashi ronsō* 一橋論叢 44.6 (December 1960), pp. 53–72.

21. *Tzu-chih t'ung-chien* 資治通鑑 (Comprehensive mirror for aid in government), by the early Sung scholar Ssu-ma Kuang 司馬光; a massive history of China through the end of the Five Dynasties. (JAF)

22. "Kanmatsu no rejisutansu undō" 漢末のレジスタンス運動(The resistance movement at the end of the Han), *Tōyōshi kenkyū* 25.4 (March 1967), pp. 23–50; included in Kawakatsu, *Rikuchō kizokusei shakai no kenkyū.*

23. *T'oung Pao* L (1963), pp. 1–78. Translated by Kawakatsu Yoshio as "Kigen ni seiki no seiji-shūkyō teki undō ni tsuite" 紀元二世紀の政治宗教的道教運動について(On the Taoist political-religious movements of the 2d century A.D.), in *Dōkyō kenkyū* 道教研究 (Studies in Taoism), edited by Yoshioka Yoshitoyo 吉岡義豊 and Michel Soymié, Shōshinsha, 1967, vol. 2, pp. 5–113.

24. *San-kuo chih* 三国志 (Chronicle of the Three Kingdoms), "Wei chih" 魏志 (Chronicle of Wei), *chuan* 8, biography of Chang Lu 張魯.

25. Ko Hung 葛洪, *Pao-p'u-tzu* 抱朴子, "Nei-p'ien, wei-chih" 内篇微旨 (Inner chapters, on subtlety), Taipei: Chung-hua shu-chü, 1968, *chuan* 6, p. 3b.

26. *Tao-chieh* 道戒. (JAF)

27. See, in addition to the studies of Stein and Kawakatsu cited in notes 18 and 23 above, Ōbuchi Ninji 大淵忍爾, "Kōkin no ran to Gotobeidō" 黄巾の乱と五斗米道(The Yellow Turban rebellion and the Five Pecks of Rice), in *Iwanami kōza sekai rekishi 5: kodai 5*, pp. 23–52.

28. 宮川尚志,「六朝時代の村について」, in *Haneda hakushi shōju kinen Tōyōshi ronsō*羽田博士頌寿記念東洋史論叢(Essays on East Asian history in honor of Professor Haneda Tōru), Kyoto, Tōyōshi kenkyūkai, 1950; included in Miyakawa's *Rikuchō shi kenkyū, seiji shakai hen* 六朝史研究政治社会篇 (Studies in Six Dynasties history, volume on political and social problems), Gakujutsu shinkōkai, 1956, pp. 437–471.

29. Miyazaki Ichisada 宮崎市定, "Chūgoku ni okeru shūraku keitai no hensen ni tsuite"中国における聚落形体の変遷について(On changes in the configurations of centers of population in China), *Ōtani shigaku* 大谷史学 6 (June 1957), pp. 5–26.

30. 那波利貞,「塢主攷」, *Shisō* 史窓 30 (October 1971), pp. 68–104; originally published in *Tō-A jimbun gakuhō* 東亜人文学報3.4 (March 1943).

31. Chin Fa-ken 金発根, *Yung-chia luan hou pei-fang te hao-tsu* 永嘉乱後北方的豪族(Great clans in the North following the uprising of 307 A.D.), Taipei, Chung-kuo hsüeh-shu chu-tso chiang-chu wei-yüan-hui, 1964.

32. Lao Kan 労幹, ed., *Chü-yen Han-chien k'ao-shih* 居廷漢簡考釈 (A study of the Han wood strips of Chü-yen), Taipei, Academia Sinica, 1960.

33. 太行. A large mountain range in Honan, Hopei, and Shansi. (JAF)

34. *Hou-Han-shu, chuan* 47, biography of Feng I 馮異.

35. 水経注 by Li Tao-yüan 酈道元 (d. 527).

36. *Shui-ching-chu, chuan* 15, entry on the Lo River I-ho 一合.

37. Ibid.

38. Ch'en Yin-k'o 陳寅恪, "T'ao-hua yüan chi p'ang-cheng" 桃花源記旁証 (Notes on the *T'ao-hua yüan chi*), *Ch'ing-hua hsüeh-pao* 清華学報 11.1 (January 1936), pp. 79–88. T'ang Ch'ang-ju 唐長孺 has written a critique of Ch'en's theory: "Tu 'T'ao-hua yüan chi p'ang-cheng' chih-i" 読桃花源記旁証質疑 (Doubts after reading [Ch'en Yin-k'o's] "Notes on the T'ao-hua yüan chi"), in *Wei Chin Nan-Pei-ch'ao shih lun-ts'ung hsü-pien* 魏晋南北朝史論叢続編(Essays on the history of the Wei, Chin, and Nan-pei-ch'ao period, continued), Peking, San-lien shu-tien, 1959, pp. 163–174. According to T'ang, the *T'ao-hua yüan chi* took for its raw material the "communitarian" life of minority peoples of Kiangnan who had fled from the feudal oppression of the Han dynasty to a place of seclusion. He goes on to claim that what Ch'en saw as the model for *T'ao-hua yüan chi*, the *wu* groups in the North led by great Han Chinese clan members, included within them feudal class relations, and that it differs greatly from seeing the *T'ao-hua yüan chi* as describing a world free of exploitation and classes. Yet, Ch'en also, drawing on the example of Yü Kun, recognized that the clan and local village structures that gave the *wu* grouping its organization possessed a "communitarian" tinge to a certain extent, and that in the early period of the group's activities it was necessary to have cooperation and mutual aid among the constituent members of the group.

39. *San-kuo chih*三国志, "Wei chih" 魏志 (Chronicle of Wei), *chuan* 11.

40. *Tsung-tsu chi shu-hsing* 宗族及庶姓, in *Chin-shu* 晋書, *chuan* 88, "hsiao-yu" 孝友.

41. *Tsung-tsu ji hsiang-ch'ü*宗族及郷曲, in ibid., *chuan* 67.

42. See Tanigawa, "Rikuchō kizokusei shakai no shiteki seikaku to ritsuryō taisei e no tenkai" 六朝貴族制社会の史的性格と律令休制への展開 (The historical character of society under the Six Dynasties aristocratic

system and the evolution of a legal order), *Shakai keizai shigaku* 社会経済史学 31.1–5 (1966), pp. 204–225; included in Tanigawa, *Chūgoku chūsei shakai to kyōdōtai*, pp. 147–173.

43. See the four essays included in Section II of Tanigawa's *Chūgoku chūsei shakai to kyōdōtai* (pp. 117–197):

a) "Ichi Tōyōshi kenkyūsha ni okeru genjitsu to gakumon" 一東洋史研究者における現実と学問 (Reality and scholarship for one scholar of East Asian history), originally in *Atarashii rekishigaku no tame ni* 新しい歴史学のために 68 (1961).

b) "Chūgoku kodai-shakai no seikaku ronsō" (see note 6).

c) "Rikuchō kizokusei shakai no shiteki seikaku to ritsuryō taisei e no tenkai" (see note 42).

d) "Chūgoku shi kenkyū no atarashii kadai: Hōkensei no saihyōka mondai ni furete" 中国史研究の新しい課題：封建制の再評価問題にふれて (A new problem in the study of Chinese history: On the reevaluation of feudalism), originally in *Nihon shi kenkyū* 日本史研究 94 (November 1967).

44. See Tanigawa, "'Kyōdōtai' ronsō ni tsuite: Chūgoku shi kenkyū ni okeru shisō jōkyō" 共同体論争について：中国史研究における思想状況 (On the *kyōdōtai* [community] debate: The state of thought in Chinese historical studies), *Nagoya jimbun kagaku kenkyūkai nempō* 名古屋人文科学研究会年報 I (1974), pp. 65–90.

45. See, in particular, Tanigawa, "Hokuchō kizoku no seikatsu rinri" 北朝貴族の生活倫理 (The life ethic of the aristocracy in the Northern Dynasties), in *Chūgoku chūsei shi kenkyū: Rikuchō Zui Tō no shakai to bunka*, pp. 272–303; included in Tanigawa, *Chūgoku chūsei shakai to kyōdōtai*, pp. 201–234.

46. *Pei-shih* 北史, *chuan* 32.

47. *Wei-shu* 魏書, *chuan* 47; *Pei-shih*, *chuan* 30.

48. *Pei-shih*, *chuan* 33.

49. *Pei-Ch'i-shu* 北斉書 (History of the Northern Ch'i), *chuan* 23; *Pei-shih*, *chuan* 24, biography of Ts'ui Ling.

50. 顔氏家訓, "Mien-hsüeh p'ien" 勉学篇 (To encourage study). (See Teng Ssu-yü's excellent annotated translation, *Family Instructions for the Yen Clan*, Leiden: E. J. Brill, 1968, pp. 52–84—JAF.)

51. Yoshikawa Tadao 吉川忠夫, "Gan Shisui shōron" 顔之推小論 (A short study of Yen Chih-t'ui), *Tōyōshi kenkyū* 20.4 (March 1962), pp. 1–29.

52. See Teng, p. 59, for a slightly different translation. (JAF)

53. *Pei-shih*, *chuan* 33.

54. See Tanigawa, *Zui-Tō teikoku keisei shiron*, sections I and II.

55. See Tanigawa, "Kindensei no rinen to dai tochi shoyū" 均田制の理念と大土地所有 (The principles of the equitable field system and large landownership), *Tōyōshi kenkyū* 25.4 (March 1967), pp. 76–97; included in Tanigawa, *Chūgoku chūsei shakai to kyōdōtai*, pp. 256–280.

56. See note 18 to Part I above for a description of *chan-t'ien* and *k'e-t'ien*. (JAF)

57. See Tanigawa, *Zui-Tō teikoku keisei shiron*, section II.

58. Ibid.

59. See Tanigawa, "So Shaku no Rikujō shōsho ni tsuite" 蘇綽の六条詔書 (Su Ch'o's Edict on six reforms), *Nagoya daigaku bungakubu kenkyū ronshū* 45 名古屋大学文学部研究論集, "shigaku" 15 史学 (1967), pp. 53–66; reprinted as "Seigi 'Rikujō shōsho' ni okeru shitaifu rinri" 西魏六条詔書における士大夫倫理 (The literary ethic in the "Edict of six articles" of the Western Wei), in Tanigawa, *Chūgoku chūsei shakai to kyōdōtai*, pp. 235–255.

Index

xi–xiv, xvii–xviii, xix, xx, xxi,
xxii, xxiv, xxvi, xxxviii, 5–53;
slavery in, 6; warrior class in,
7
Japan-United States Hakone
Conference, 42
Jurchen-Chin era, 63

Kaizuka Shigeki, 76, 78
Kao Huan, 115
Katō Shigeshi, 6–7, 9, 11, 14, 44
Kawachi Jōzō, xxv
Kawakatsu Yoshio, xvi, xix,
xxii, xxv, xxvi, xxvii, xxviii,
xxix; on aristocracy, 96; on
community, xxi; on Pure
Stream, 91–93, 94, 95, 96, 97,
98; on Six Dynasties, xxi; on
Yellow Turbans, 99
Kiangnan, xvi
Kobayashi Yoshiaki, xiii
Ko Hung, 101
Kuan-chung of Ch'i, 78, 79
K'ung Kuang, 90
Kuwabara Takeo, xiii
Kyōdōtai. See Community/
communitarianism
Kyoto School, xvii, 31, 32, 36.
See also Naitō Konan

Land: allocation, 122–124;
annexation, 89–91;
assessment, 15, 123;
borrowed, 14; and class, 123;
ownership of, 31, 56, 111,
122–124; in possession, 15,
123. *See also* Equitable field
system
Landlord system, 25–26, 28, 30,
31, 33. *See also*
Tenancy/tenant farming
Legalists, 79–80, 81, 86
Leningrad Conference of 1931,
53
Liang family, 90
Li An-shih, 123
Li Hsiao-chen, 114
Li Hsien, 104

Ling, Emperor, 90
Ling, Empress, 113
Literati, 37, 107, 108;
associations of, 92; and
community, 111; decline of,
125; evaluations of, 91–92,
111; ethic, xxii, 93–94, 97–
98, 108, 111, 124, 125; in
Latter Han, 89, 94–95;
learning for, 116, 118–119.
See also Eremites; Pure
Stream literati
Li Tzu-hsiung, 118
Li Tzu-tan, 118–119
Liu Pang, 14, 83; Three Articles
of Law of, 84, 85
Liu Yü, 105
Lu I-hsi, 113, 114, 115, 118
Lung-hsi, 104

Maeda Naonori, 11–12
Mantetsu, xi
Marxism/Marxist historians,
54; and Asiatic mode of
production, 50, 52, 57,
58–59; on China, xi–xii,
xiv–xv, xix, xx–xxi, xxiv,
xxvi; class concept of history
of, xxiii; v. modernization
theory, 41, 42; and non-
European societies, 55; and
periodization, xii; v. Weber,
xx
Masubuchi Tatsuo, xiv, 43, 78,
81; on Pure Stream, 93–94,
95, 96, 97, 98
Maternal relatives, 90, 97;
power of, 91, 100
Matsumoto Shinhachirō, 12
Ma Yüan, 104
Medieval period, xvii–xviii, xix,
xxv, 10, 24, 31, 32, 36, 89; in
Japan, 6
Meiji Restoration, xii, xiii, 42
Men of Filial Piety and
Incorruptibility, 86
Military, xvi–xvii, xxiii, 7, 17–
18, 125–126

Designer:	U.C. Press Staff
Compositor:	Asco Trade Typesetting Ltd.
Printer:	Edwards Bros., Inc.
Binder:	Edwards Bros., Inc.
Text:	10/12 Times Roman
Display:	Times Roman

DATE DUE			

Tanigawa   200901